TINT[illegible]RY

Researched & Edited by Judith Russill

DEDICATED TO ALL RESIDENTS OF CHAPEL HILL AND TINTERN PARVA - PAST AND PRESENT

ACKNOWLEDGEMENTS

This book has been produced and published by the Parochial Church Council, St Michaels' Church, Tintern. The publishers believe the information contained in this book to be correct, but do not hold themselves responsible for inaccuracies.

The Editor particularly wishes to acknowledge the assistance given by Miss Anne Rainsbury of The Chepstow Museum, and Mr and Mrs Eric Wiles. She is also extremely grateful for information and the loan of photographs from Mr Henry Arnold, Mrs Madge Cowell, Mr and Mrs Winston Evans, Mr David Ford, Mr and Mrs Paul Hayward, Miss D Heath, Mrs Betty Hoskins, Mrs G Hubbard, Mr and Mrs Sid Jones, Mrs Dorothy Lawrence, Mr W J Pickering, Mr and Mrs Douglas Phillips, Mrs Ann Smith, Miss Margery Thomas, Mr R Townsend, Mr R S Waite, Mr and Mrs E D Wheeler, Mr and Mrs H Woolfson, The Royal Commission on Ancient and Historical Buildings in Wales, and to all others who offered advice, encouragement and forbearance. And, finally, thanks to Mrs Elaine Dollery, Mr Frank Keys, Mr Adrian Smith, and the Rector, The Rev. Julian E.Ll. White, B.A., who managed to interpret and embellish the Editors' notes and instructions and write their spendid articles.

ALL PROFITS FROM THIS BOOK TO BE DONATED TO THE RESTORATION FUND OF ST MICHAELS', TINTERN.

Cover photograph, "Siesta", by Mr R S Waite

Published 1990 Reprinted June 1991

ISBN 0 9516010 0 8 Tinterns' Story Paperback

Introduction

In the August of 1986 I found myself many thousands of miles away from Tintern in the town of Fredericksburg, Virginia. At that time it must be confessed this distance was little more than a cold statistic in my mind as I was "between parishes" as it were.

I was taking a working vacation in the U.S.A. having left one parish to shortly take up, at the request of the Archbishop of Wales, the living of Llandogo, Whitebrook and Tintern.

This particular morning, at the unholy hour of 7.30 am, I found myself addressing some sixty Rotarians at a Power Breakfast in a splendid restaurant whose decor proudly boasted the essence of Southern elegance.

By way of a starting point, I introduced myself as a native of Wales and enquired whether any of the company knew the geographical location of this Celtic heartland.

A deathly hush followed, broken at length by a hesitant drawl venturing the possibility that Wales was "somewhere near London". With reflection, and learning something of the distance the average U.S. male travels daily, I suppose the answer was not incorrect. In the situation however I was becoming desperate to strike a more responsive chord with my audience as my theme was something along the lines of Celtic Religious Legacy.

I quickly hit upon the idea of asking whether any present had heard of Tintern Abbey - hardly a Celtic shrine it is true but a speaker must start somewhere. I was amazed to see a number of hands raised in acknowledgement and it transpired that not only was the ruined abbey identifiable but also had been visited by many of the group.

Looking back at the experience I suppose it was a case of Wales Tourist Board - 0 Tintern - 1.

There is little doubt that Tintern is well and truly on the map almost exclusively on account of its magnificent abbey remains. However, since taking up my duties as Rector of the parish, I soon learned that there was a great deal more to Tintern - both past and present - than it's famous edifice.

That is the purpose of this book; to provide a researched history and flavour of the village and the immediate area, which, we feel, is often ignored in the many publications which choose solely to feature Tintern Abbey.

As a new-comer to Tintern, I am privileged to be in a position where I have access to a variety of historical records relating to the village and, just as importantly, the good fortune to converse with residents who recall the community from their youth and who are part of the present structure. These are the voices who will be leading you on a fascinating journey in the following pages.

A special word of appreciation must be extended to Miss Judith Russill. This volume is in no small part a tribute to her genuine love of the village and to her unquenchable enthusiasm and diligent research. She has undertaken the daunting task of compiling this book with zeal and dedication and I simply commend it to you without reservation.

Tintern has been kind to me. It is an area of outstanding beauty and history, and it also provided me with a wife. Kate is the Head Custodian of Tintern Abbey (I could have done with her back in Virginia) and, for me, there is a comfortable irony in the remark made by the present Bishop of Monmouth who, speaking shortly after officiating at our wedding, suggested that Kate was now responsible for looking after two ruins.

I am confident that monastic ruin of Tintern and Judith Russill's book will wear better that this ruinous Clerk in Holy Orders.

Julian E.Ll. White Rector

TINTERN'S HISTORY

By Judith Russill

Because of the dearth of written, and sparsity of visual evidence about early Tintern, one can be forgiven for assuming that little happened in this valley prior to the arrival of the monks in 1131. However, we do know something about events in the neighbourhood from early times onwards, and from this we are able to deduce that man has known about and visited Tintern for some considerable time before the 12th century.

There are two natural phenomena about the valley without which the village would not have existed. Firstly, the River Wye has provided the means of food, transport and industrial power, and secondly, the heavily forested hills have provided fuel, cover for game, berries and fruits. Early man has hunted in South East Wales from the end of the Ice Age, and paleolithic artifacts have been found near Chepstow. But, closer to home, the first real evidence we have is that Bronze Age man frequented the area (around BC2000), and one of them left a hoard of six Breton socketed axes buried in a field on the extreme edge of Chapel Hill parish, at Livox Farm. Axes were highly valued, so to find six together is quite exceptional. In 1926, they were deposited at the National Museum of Wales, Cardiff, but casts can be seen at the museum attached to Tintern Abbey. It is not difficult to imagine our hunter-gatherer forbears setting traps for animals in the woods, or crouching over the Angidy River trying to catch trout! Whether they actually settled in the valley, or were foraging parties from settlements nearby, we shall probably never know.

From this period, we move on to the Iron Age, and by now, the Celtic peoples were beginning to enter the British Isles. Slowly, various tribes evolved, and by the time the Romans had reached the River Severn, in AD47, they were confronted by the tribe of the Silures. This tribe occupied an area roughly corresponding to the counties of Gwent and Glamorgan, and they put up a spirited resistance to the Romans, and it took well over thirty years before they were brought to heel. In 1969, Mr Ralph Hodges, the Headmaster of Tintern School, found in his garden an iron-age Celtic coin of the Dubonni. The Dubonni were the neighbouring tribe to the Silures, occupying the territory east of the Wye, and although it is not unusual to find trading between two tribes, this find is of particular interest, as the Welsh Celtic tribes were not coin-users. The coin is now on permanent display at the Museum in Cardiff.

The area now known as Tintern would have been familiar to the Roman troops during their first few years occupying Wales. Until they built a wooden bridge at Chepstow, the Romans used the ford at Tintern as one of their crossing places over the Wye on their journeys from Gloucester to the forts as Usk and Caerleon. The site of this ford has always been open to question, but it would seem that the most obvious place is just upstream of the railway bridge. It would have been a short march from there to the Roman road above the Angidy Valley. Various Roman artifacts have been unearthed in the village, a brooch being found on the Roman road itself, and near Pont-y-Saeson, a hoard of Romano-British remains were uncovered. This is now at the British Museum, having been purchased in 1891 from W Edkins, Esq. The hoard numbers some 134 items, including three enamelled fibulae of the early 2nd Century AD, and four enamelled disc fibulae. A small Roman coin hoard, dating from around AD270, (found in the village) is now held at the National Museum in Cardiff. It has been suggested that there might have been a Roman Villa at Tintern,and certainly, on the site of the Abbey itself, there has been found the remains of a Romano-British settlement. No doubt, whilst Tintern was used as a crossing point, there must have been some early ancestor earning a living by supplying the needs of the traveller, just as they do today!

From the start of the fourth century, the Romans began withdrawing their armies from Britain, and this continued during that century. The growing threat, presented by the invading Saxons, meant that the tribes, without their Roman overlords, had to organize themselves in order to defend their country. During the late 5th and early 6th centuries, the area now known as Wales became more and more isolated from the rest of the peoples of Britain, and from this time the Cymry began to develop as a separate people and culture. So, the Kingdom of Gwent emerged, and the next evidence we have of Tintern's history is towards the end of the 6th century. The King of Gwent, Tewdrig, a great warrior, decided to end his days as a hermit, living amongst the rocks of Tintern. It is possible that from this time the village gained its' name, as the meaning is from the Welsh "din", (hill or fort) and "teyrn" (king), hence the Hill of the King. However, poor Tewdrig was not to end his days in peaceful contemplation. His son, Meurig, faced with the threat of Saxon invasion from across the Wye, realised that their only hope of success was to be led into battle by the great Tewdrig. The Saxons crossed the river and were engaged in battle by the Welsh, who defeated them soundly at Tintern. Still, to this day, the battle is recorded,as at the top of the Angidy valley is a bridge known as Pont y Saeson, "Bridge of the Saxons". Despite saving the day, Tewdrig was mortally wounded, and was taken to Mathern, where he died. The legend states that he was carried from the battlefield in a cart drawn by two stags, and at each stopping place, a spring of clear water flowed, in order to bathe his wounds. Springs can still be found along the route!

The Lower Wye Valley, from late Roman times, had a strong Christian tradition, and locally there were two leading Celtic Churches (or Clas), at Llandogo and Caerwent. The earliest reference to a church at Llandogo is in AD625, and by AD 765, a church had been established at Tintern.

Less than twenty years after this date, Offa, King of Mercia, began his major building project - Offa's Dyke. This was to run the length of the border, between England and Wales, but whether it was built for defensive purposes or purely for demarcation is a matter open for debate. Here, at Tintern, the Dyke is on the Gloucestershire side of the Wye, but the people who had by now settled in the valley would have been aware of the Mercian officials surveying the area, and, maybe some of the locals were coerced into constructing the Dyke itself!

During this period, it would have become evident that the Celtic peoples living west of the Wye were a quite different race from the Anglo Saxons now inhabiting England. Whereas the English language was evolving, the old Celtic tongue was still to be heard in what was to become Wales, and although Wales was broken into several kingdoms, there was a common form of government. Each kingdom was divided into several large administrative units called a cantref, which, originally had been based on one hundred (cant) townships (trefydd). The cantref was subdivided into smaller units, called Cymydau, to make easier the collection of dues and for the holding of courts. Twice a year, the king would travel around his realm (gwlad) and stay in each district for three days in order to hear appeals, and no doubt check the administrative machinery. The freemen donated the food and drink, and the bondsmen supplied the fuel and some food. In time, these progresses became less frequent, so the food dues were commuted, and instead, money payments were made, thus starting a system of taxation. Gwent consisted of 3 cantref. Tintern was in the Cantref of Is Coed, and the Cymydau was Trellech. Until the last century, the local administration area was still known as the Hundred of Trellech. The next invaders to arrive in the British Isles were the Vikings, and even they would have been seen in Tintern, as their longboats reached Monmouth. Fear apart, that must have been a splendid spectacle - it is not difficult to imagine a long boat emerging from the mists on the river on a chill autumn morning.

There is a 9th century reference to Tintern, in the Liber Landavensis. This concerns the purchase of land by Cynfelin, son of Cynog, from Rhodri, son of Ithel (any connection, I wonder, to the woods on the edge of the neighbouring parish of Llandogo called Coed Ithel?) The area referred to as the land of Louhai is defined thus:

> *"the influx of the Catfrut (Catbrook) into the Wye along it upwards directly opposite to the ridge of Tintern, to the cliff, upwards to the ridge of Tintern, from the ridge of Tintern downwards to the Wye, along the Wye and its weirs to the influx of Catfrut where it began".*

Thus we come to the invasion of the Normans, and by 1067, the eastern parts of Wales had already been parcelled out amongst the Norman Lords. Chepstow and area was under the lordship of William FitzOsbern, and it was his family that founded the Abbey in Tintern. Within ten years of the Battle of Hastings, in 1066, the Normans had seen the need to subdue the unruly Welsh, and thus began an oppressive regime that was to last four hundred years.

There began a series of uprisings and wars against the Normans. The first of the great leaders being Owain Gwynedd and the Lord Rhys. By the end of the 12th Century, Llywelen ap Iorwerth, grandson of Owain, had taken up the gauntlet, and by the middle of the 1200s his grandson, Llywelen ap Gruffydd was confronting the English King. However, most of these campaigns were conducted westwards of Brecon and in the North, so it is unlikely that Tintern saw much of these events, but would have been aware of the turmoil.

Tintern Abbey was often visited by the nobility, so the village would have been well aware of the world outside the valley. There were burials of leading figures, particularly of the Pembroke family. The Countess, Isabel, was buried in 1220, and her sons, Walter and Anselm both in 1246. These sad events would have taken place with some pomp, and no doubt large numbers would have attended. Another visitor to the Abbey was the King himself. The various Welsh revolts were not the only problems for the English. In early 1320, there was opposition and revolt against the King. In his efforts to hold onto his throne, Edward II chose Chepstow Castle to be the site of his last stand, and he arrived in Tintern on the 13th October, 1326, where he stayed for two nights, before continuing to Chepstow. The final attempt by the Welsh for independence was spearheaded by Owain Glyndwr, and towards the close of the 14th Century, he managed to gather most of the Welsh into the nearest thing to a national force that had been seen. Initially, the Welsh were very successful, but, bit by bit the English regained control, and by 1415, Glyndwr had disappeared from the scene. But not before his forces had come very close to home. In 1404 he successfully fought a battle at Craig y Dorth, on the outskirts of Monmouth. He also attacked Trellech, then one of the major towns in Wales. It has been suggested that the weirs along the Wye, belonging to the Abbey, were destroyed at about this time by Glyndwr's supporters. In 1401/2 the abbot petitioned the King and referred to his "poor House of Tintern", and in November 1406, in a letter to the Bishop of Hereford, the King states that "the greater part of the Abbey and all its goods had been destroyed and consumed by the Welsh rebels".

Another threat during this period was the Black Death, which had reached East Gwent in the spring and early summer of 1349. It is believed that the neighbouring parish of Penterry was decimated in this way, though we have no definite proof that it reached Tintern. But the Abbey had to radically reorganise the running of its estates because of a drastic loss of manpower, and the court roll of Porthcasseg for July 31, 1349, indicates six deaths in the area - an abnormally high figure.

It is often assumed that the Abbey existed on its' own in the valley. But there is considerable evidence to show that alongside the monastery had developed a secular community, including shopkeepers, in nearby Chapel Hill and up the Angidy Valley. In 1447, there is mention of cottages near the Abbey gate. Jenkin Gwyneth is recorded as having built, in 1457, a new mansion on Chapel Hill. Various trades and traders are mentioned: in 1442, William Vaughan was given permission to sell bread, ale and merchandise, and both Richard Gruffydd and Hywell Rogers sold meat. The address of two "locals", Thomas Hayward and John Glass, is given as "of the Abbey" in 1447, and in 1506, John Whitmyll of the Lower Angidy Valley was granted a licence to sell bread and wine. John Potley and the lessee of the Angidy Mill were also allowed to sell bread, ale and other merchandise in 1524. The original church of Chapel Hill, St Mary's, is mentioned as early as 1131, and no doubt was to serve the spiritual needs of the ordinary people living outside the confines of the Abbey. Many local people would have been employed by the

Abbey as woodsmen, herdsmen and to undertake the more menial tasks around the many farms.

1485 saw the Battle of Bosworth, and the part-Welsh Henry Tudor acquired the English throne. But it was the actions of his son, Henry VIII that were to have such a far reaching impact on Tintern. By 1536, he had decided on the Dissolution of the Monasteries, and on the 3rd September, 1536, Tintern Abbey and all its granges were handed over to the Crown. Having taken all the valuables, the estates were granted by the Crown, to Charles Herbert, Earl of Worcester in 1537. This family were to dominate the area until the Duke of Beaufort relinquished much of the land to the Crown in 1901. By 1541, the lead from the Abbey roof had gone, and so the abbey began to crumble away, encouraged by forays of the locals wanting building materials for their houses. I doubt that there are many houses in the village built before the last century that do not have some part of the Abbey in their fabric!

It was a time of enormous change for the villagers - many ran businesses, shops, mills and the like, that were dependent on the Abbey and its visitors. The few remaining monks, twelve in number, and the Abbot, Richard Wyche, were pensioned off. John Gethin became curate of Newnham and Nicholas Acton eventually became perpetual curate of Hewelsfield. The others (Maurice Burnell, Richard Wade, Robert Thomas, Thomas Elliotts, Thomas Piell, Thomas Robyns, Thomas Tintern, William Gloucester, William Hopkins and William Machyn), received dispensation from their religious vows and were permitted to wear secular habit. It would be interesting to know if any remained in the village!

That could have been the end for Tintern, but for an amazing stroke of luck. The Crown was needful of brass and iron for ordnance, and started looking for a suitable area where they could establish a foundry. The original site was to be near Bristol, but the necessary river proved too sluggish, so the engineers, being in the area, decided to explore to see if a better site could be found. They came into the Lower Wye Valley, and discovered that Tintern could offer all that was needed - fuel, fast flowing water, a navigable river for transportation, and nearby, the necessary minerals. In 1568, the Society of Mineral and Battery Works was founded, and so began Tintern's industrial life. There is evidence that, in medieval times, copper and lead were being smelted within the Abbey precincts, and recent excavations found much to support this. By 1570, a brass and wire factory had started in Chapel Hill, and the Wire Works were to dominate the two parishes of Chapel Hill and Tintern Parva for the next three hundred years, becoming the principal employers in the area.

None of the major battles of the Civil War took place near Tintern, but there were skirmishes and both Monmouth and Chepstow fell to the Parliamentarians in 1645 and 1646. Although the main landowner was a Royalist, the Earl of Worcester, the Manor, at Tintern Parva, was the home of Lewis Morris, related to the Morris' of Piercefield. The story goes that the Manor was destroyed by Parliamentarian forces, but if the house was owned by Lewis Morris, this seems to be unlikely. Maybe it was the Royalists who were responsible for the sacking. It was during this war, that Prince Rupert, commander of the King's Cavalry arrived in the area, and there is a local story that Rupert, anxious to obtain as many horses as possible for the Army, travelled from Chepstow up the valley to see what he could requisition. However, to the villagers of Tintern, a horse was a valuable commodity, both as a means of transport and as a source of haulage power, particularly for dragging timber from out of the forests. So, the tale relates, they took their horses and disappeared into the surrounding forests, thus avoiding Rupert as he rode through! Although the Earl of Worcester lost his estates during the Commonwealth, they were restored to him following the Restoration of Charles II. As time passed, the Wire Works continued to expand, and little else is known to have happened in the village over the next hundred years. But by the middle of the 18th Century, as government administration became more organised, we find that more and more records were made, and are still available. Registering of ships became necessary, and these records provide us with valuable insight into the variety and size of vessels that sailed up and down the Wye. It must be remembered that there was still no direct route to Tintern overland, as the route of the main road as we know it today did not appear until the 1820's. Chepstow was connected to Monmouth by the road that went over the top ridge, above Tintern, passing through Devauden. Travellers to Tintern had to leave this road, and pass through Porthcasseg and Penterry and then down into the valley on the old coach road behind the Beaufort Hotel. The road known today as Chapel Lane was the original road to follow, and led to the river side by the lower mill. Having passed along the village, much as it does today, it then left via a lane to the right of the Wye Valley Hotel, through Parva Farm, behind the Nurtons, and then dropping down to Coed Ithel.

The most major event to affect Britain and Europe towards the end of the 18th century was the war fought against Napoleon and France. Even this momentous occurrence was to affect Tintern.

During the 18th century it had been the custom of the wealthy to send their sons on a Grand Tour of Europe as part of their education. The War, however put paid to this, and books written by individual travellers in Britain made people aware that this country too had much to offer by way of grand scenery and beautiful buildings. Thus tours of Tintern Abbey and the beautiful Wye Valley increased and the beginnings of a profitable tourism industry were born. There had been many inns and hotels in Tintern, catering for the thirst of the wire workers, but as this trade began to slacken, during the last century, so the tourists arrived, thus ensuring that some of the inns had a good future. Just as it is today, tourism became a major employer in the valley. The various census', from 1841 onwards, show that many were employed as servants, ostlers, lodging house keepers, laundresses, publicans and so on.

The building of the new road, connecting Chepstow to Monmouth, via St Arvans, Tintern and Llandogo, made travelling much easier, and "day trips" to Tintern became possible. The railway arrived in 1876, a station being built just one mile north of the village thus increasing tourism. The wire works industry began to decline, and even the building of a branch line with a bridge across the Wye, into the heart of Chapel Hill, failed to revitalise the Works, and by the end of the nineteenth century, they had finally closed. Many of the old workers cottages fell into disrepair, and as the population began to drop, they were left to crumble away. But in the latter half of the last century many of the houses that we recognise today were built. The Beaufort Estates built cottages for their foresters and farm workers, and the easier access to the village by transport made the prospect of retirement to Tintern an attractive one. The village school was built, both the churches rebuilt and the Methodist Chapel was erected down on the Quay. Tintern acquired a Post Office and a Policeman. The Church Rooms became a focus of village life and the numerous Directories published, made much of the Surpliced Choir leading the Church services! The football team was started. We still have a football team, but the choir has gone! The school has closed, and the policeman removed, but we now have a Vineyard! A number of the pubs have closed, but there is still plenty of choice for visitors and villagers alike. Tintern sent its young men to both the World Wars, and some came home. The older villagers remember splendid Pageants - the British Legion Parades, before the last War, were something to behold, and the Horticultural Shows were huge events. Tents were erected on the Leytons and there were many classes to enter and prizes and cups to be won. Races for the children, and a day packed with events. In recent years the Horticultural show has been revived, but on a much smaller scale and with a different name. Recently, the Carnival has been held again where all the village "pull together" to produce a very happy afternoon. To finance this event, the committee hold a Duck Race on Easter Monday. Where once the Wye was full of trading and pleasure craft, it comes alive again with a thousand yellow ducks valiantly fighting the currents as they swim downstream. Some get trapped by the banks, so, for a few hours the river appears to be lined with daffodils, when viewed from afar! Although there are many newcomers now living in Tintern, most are no longer dependent on the village for their livelihood, it is good that there are still a considerable number who are descendants of people who lived here three hundred years ago.

Thus ends this history of Tintern. Despite the shortage of information about the village's past, I hope that by relating what history we do know about the area to the well known historical events of the country as a whole, it has been shown that a community has lived and worked in this parish since time immemorial and has played its small part in life's rich pattern.

ONCE UPON A TIME

By Rose M Jones

Looking through an old magazine, I chanced upon the "Diary of a Harassed Housewife", by June Smith, and it set me thinking back to the days when my sons were small and there was shopping to be done.

No harassed housewife here - hardest job to find something to put on my shopping list - rations and shortages prevailed. Every Friday morning this was done, I had simply to cross the road and place my order on the counter at "Aubrey's", and later, that same day, the goods were placed on my kitchen table. Do not think that I was a privileged customer - this was the norm for all his customers.

"Aubrey's" was the General Store in the Trellech Road, now a private house - "Orchards". It was owned and run by Mr Aubrey Williams, a bachelor, with occasional help from his housekeeper, Miss Holmes. The store was quite unique, literally a *general* store.

Mr Williams had served an apprenticeship with a tailor in Cardiff and had seen service with the Royal Navy in the 14/18 War before returning home to look after the family business, his father having died previously. It was, therefore, possible for the men of the village to be measured for a new suit, and many were, and to get a complete outfit including shoes or boots. Ladies, too, were catered for.

All kinds of groceries were stocked; matured cheeses were a speciality, bread (not his mother's home baking, this had been discontinued), bacon, sweets, all tinned goods, fresh fruit and Corona drinks. Indeed it was almost impossible to ask for something he hadn't got. There were animal and chicken feeds, paraffin, methylated spirits for primus stoves and Tilley lamps (no mod cons in those days). Stationery, mantles and prickers, candles, cigarettes, tobacco, matches, lamp glasses, the list was endless. There were also various medications including embrocation (double strength) - honestly. Household goods were stocked too.

No doubt there are readers who will remember a host of other things. No self service in that store - just ordered chaos, but that wise owner literally knew where everything was. When there was not room in the shop for things, they were kept either in the back or up in the loft, via a step ladder. If something was wanted from the outside, he would trot off out of the shop and invariably return with the goods. Meanwhile, customers waited patiently for their turn to be served, silently hoping no-one else would want something from upstairs.

The shop opened at 8.00 am prompt and closed at 7.00 pm, Monday to Saturday. Thursday was half-day closing. Promptly at 2.00 pm, the pony had been harnessed and hitched to the cart, then loaded with orders for Trellech Road and Botany Bay (no estate houses then), and Mr Williams went on his round to place more goods on kitchen tables.

No numbers on screens in those days, no serve yourself and amazing as it may seem today, no delivery charges!

Although there were three other grocery shops in the village, there was only one "Aubrey's".

[EDITORS NOTE: Aubrey Williams died in 1968, and his ashes are interred in his parents', Francis and Edith, grave. Next to this is the grave of Aubrey's grandparents, Valentine and Ellen Williams. Valentine, born at Tidenham, ran a successful carpentry business in Tintern Parva, as, according

to the Post Office Directory for 1871, he had been "elevated" to the rank of gentry! The Williams family were descended from the Marshes, a family that had lived in Chapel Hill parish for many generations.]

TINTERN'S INDUSTRY

By Frank Keys

We now left the great road at the village of Treleg, and passed through hollow and uncouth tracks, seldom attempted by any carriage but those of the natives. After a few specimens of pleasing recluse scenery, we enter a profound dell for several miles; a gurgling brook winding through the umbrageous cavity which supplies a number of large iron works above the village of Abbey-Tintern. Mr Tanner is the ostensible manager; the Duke of Beaufort the great proprietor. We inspected the principal furnace, and saw the ore, which is mostly brought from the vast source at Furness, in Lancashire, dissolved by the blasts of immense bellows, worked upon the modern construction of cylinder pumps. They have a method of separating the best qualities from the dross, by a water wheel and hammers, from which they collect considerable quantities of pure metal, and the powder sells to the glass houses for their use. Lower down are various forges, for purpose of striking this mutilated ore, into every requisite size and form of the broadest bars to the finest wires.

William Gilpin (from "Tintern Abbey" by Charles Heath, 1793)

It is almost impossible for twentieth century travellers, coming to Tintern from any direction, to realise that they are entering a former industrial area. But such it was for over three and a half centuries, the principal activites being the smelting and forging of iron, wire drawing and tinplate manufacturing. These continued right down to the turn of the century.

It had long been thought that the monks themselves brought iron making here, along with copper and lead smelting, and this was borne out in 1979 when an archaeological "dig" in the Abbey precincts (next to the ruins of the guest house) revealed evidence of forges, furnaces, kilns and metal slag. This may well be the unidentified spot where, according to a plaque on the Abbey wall, "In 1568 brass was first made by alloying copper with zinc".

But, to return to the iron industry . . . . It was the need of the burgeoning woollen industry in the time of the first Queen Elizabeth for high quality wire, for the "cards" used for combing the wool prior to spinning, that put Tintern into a substantial way of business. British wire at that time was hand drawn and inferior to the machine drawn Continental variety. Sensibly, it was Government policy to make the country less dependent on imports and so, in 1566 William Humfrey, Assay Master of the Royal Mint, and a German "expert" Christopher Schutz decided upon Tintern in which to set up the first water powered wireworks in Britain, their first mill having no less than six wheels.

The project, unfortunately, had a disastrous start because Schutz and his German workers proved, in the event, to know little or nothing of wire making. In modern parlance, they brought off a classic "con". What they did know was how to make brass, and this they proceeded to do. Thus, almost by accident, Tintern became the first place in Britain where brass objects were cast, giving it the lead in this branch of technical development.

The wire making situation was saved by recruiting another German who really knew what he was about and, with other Elizabethan entrepreneurs joining in, the "Society of Mineral and Battery Works" was launched in 1568.

Tintern proved an ideal site with unlimited water power available from the Angidy River(which joins the Wye just below the railway bridge); power which is much in evidence even today though, alas, all going to waste. There were, moreover, ample supplies of that other essential, timber for charcoal making. The iron itself was at first brought in from outside the area, though from a forge owned by the Society.

It had to be a special kind of iron called "osmond" which lent itself to the stretching and manipulating necessary in the wire drawing process - what the experts call "ductility".

It is not known just when the Directors recognised the obvious benefits of having their furnaces and forges also in the Angidy valley, but we do know that by 1672 some 1,000 tons of pig iron were being produced per year in the local furnace and that at least two, probably three, forges were at work preparing it for the wireworks by 1690, as well as producing merchant and bar iron for other purposes. When it is realised that the production of each ton of iron required 190 bushels of charcoal, the need for ample supplies of timber will be obvious. In fact, the rapid decimation of the forests was soon causing alarm, and this was well before the days when a single warship would use up 2,000 tons.

By this time, 120 Tintern workers were engaged in both the iron, wire and brass industries (total wages were £18 per week). Another record (1597) estimates that 5,000 workers all over the country were manufacturing all kinds of goods, from needles to birdcages, from the supplies of wire for which Tintern held the monopoly.

In the early days, transport was either by packhorse or by the River Wye which gave easy access to the flourishing port of Chepstow. Iron ore came from the Forest of Dean to Brockweir, just upstream of Tintern, where it was loaded onto barges. To facilitate the shipping of both incoming and outgoing goods, a small floating dock was constructed in 1693, where the Angidy joins the main river, and this can be seen to this day. As the tide at Tintern has a rise and fall of over twenty feet, it had gates to impound the water and their position may still be seen. There were also quays along the bank towards the Abbey.

In the wall of the dock the remains of a large water wheel have been discovered and there is a distinct possibility that this may have been the site of a tide mill. If so, it is probably unique in this part of the country.

A long period of prosperity and expansion ensued until, by the early nineteenth century (1821 to be exact) we learn that in the two miles of the Angidy Valley there were twenty wheels working and twelve dams or damned ponds to regulate their supply of water. Several "leats" (artificial channels to bring water to the wheels more effectively) were also constructed. There is an interesting map of the valley showing all of these in the exhibition building at the Abbey.

However, business did not remain at a uniformly high level and, by the middle of the century, the wireworks were in decline and the smelting furnace was closed down. Nevertheless, one prestigious order came Tintern's way in 1876, the supply of at least some part of the first trans-Atlantic telegraph cable.

The coming of the Wye Valley Railway with its spur across the river right into the works failed to produce the hoped for revival of business. Then came a general slump in the British wire industry and a change-over to tinplate manufacture was made in 1880.

By 1901, even that failed and the three hundred and fifty years of Tintern's industrial importance came to an end.

But, enough of history; let's take a walk up the Angidy Valley and discover what little remains to be seen.

1 LOWER (or ABBEY) FORGE

The main building here (now the Abbey Mill Craft Shop) is on the site of, and may well be, the Lower or Abbey Forge and on the side,by the wooded steps, may be seen the remains of the only water wheel still to be found in the entire valley. The spindle of another wheel may be seen in the opposite wall. There was also a corn mill on this site and probably at least four wheels in all. In the early days of the present century, the mill became a sawmill and wood turnery. The water supply was from a pond on the other side of the road, now mostly filled in to provide the "Royal George" car park. The main road (first constructed around 1820) is laid across the dam and obscures most of it, but by leaning over the wall at the right hand end, what looks like original stonework may be seen and timber uprights where sluice gates must have been. To the right again, an iron barred gate closes off the clearly defined railway track from the bridge to the wireworks. The Wye Valley Railway track was laid on the route of an earlier narrow gauge tramway down to the Wye. There was another siding down by the present doctor's surgery. The works had their own locomotive for use on the branch. Incidentally, the "locals" say that the rails of the level crossing are still in place beneath the road.

2 LOWER WIREWORKS.

The road at the side of the "Royal George" runs right up the Angidy Valley and, for most of the way, the river is right alongside. Just past the old village school and by the magnificent "Monkey Puzzle" tree, the entrance to a large, level site is found together with two somewhat ramshackle sheds. This is all that remains of the main wireworks which turned to tinplate and, after 1901 became a sawmill, first for stone and then for timber. The railway siding ran along by the river on the far side and it's embankmented track can be traced behind the two houses by the entrance.

The water supply was from a leat across the road where the tarmac footpath now runs. It is not clear where the original water wheels were, but in later days, water was led below the road to an underground turbine house. Look over the fence at the right hand end of the main shed and a large square cover marks the spot. In fact the turbine and control gear are still there.

Some time in the nineteenth century the water supply was supplemented by a pond on the left hand side of the road behind the long stone wall, just before the fork in the road. The pond is now silted up and overgrown but can be clearly seen after a minor scramble up the bank at the end of the pavement. In the bottom right hand corner is a stone chamber with steps going down. This was the overflow sluice, and the outflow to the river is on the other side of the road.

3 HAMMER HOUSE AND LITTLE BLOCK MILL

Nothing remains of these, but the white bungalow on the left of the road fork stands on the site.

The water for these and for the wireworks was a lengthy leat roughly on the line of the road to the left. This was, in fact, the original road up the valley; what is now the "main" road came much later. Taking the left fork, the leat itself, now a public footpath, can be picked up on the right, just past the upper entrance to the "Cherry Tree" Inn. It runs more or less at the roof level of the houses to its right and is supported on the original dry stone wall.

Rather than follow it, however, it is probably better to return to the lower road by the "Cherry Tree" steps, or those alongside the next house. Here the Angidy is right alongside the road and its power is immediately obvious, even in near drought conditions. It never stops!

4 WORKER'S HOMES

The white-fronted house, "Ty Nant", the adjoining Chapel Garage and the tall yellow "Valley House" are said to be where some of Schutz's German workers had their homes.

5 WEIR AND SLUICE FOR THE LEAT

Just past the three houses, the river tumbles over a small weir on the far side of which is the sluice, its gates still there but permanently closed. A closer look may be had by taking the footpath behind "Primrose Cottage" which actually straddles the river.

6 MIDDLE MILL AND MIDDLE TONGS MILL

The site of these is not known for certain but the most likely is the levelled site with some substantial retaining walls where there are now a pair of white cottages with Royal cypher and the date 1904. At the side of the left hand one of the pair, some very old stone steps lead up to the lane, and these could well have been the entrance.

7 CHAPEL WIRE MILL

Another artificially levelled site with retaining walls now forming the gardens of the last two cottages in the lane. The mill here was originally for corn and later for crushing oil seed. Behind the site, and some thirty feet above, is the leat, now a broad footpath leading to the very well preserved pond and dam a little further up the road. It can be followed by turning up the lane for fifty yards or so and taking the "Angidy Ironworks" path to the right. Alternatively continue up the valley on the road. But, one last look at Orchard Cottage as you pass by; the far left upstairs room is supposed to have been one of the offices for the Works.

8 TILTING MILL AND POND

Another of the same group which has disappeared, but old maps place the mill immediately below the dam of the well preserved pond to the left of the road. Substantial masonry and the arrangement of the sluices support the idea.

9 ABBEY TINTERN FURNACE

Just a little further up and on the right hand side is this most extensive and recently excavated site of the charcoal fired furnace dating from the early 1660's. Over this site was an orchard where older villagers remember playing on their way home from school! With the aid of two information panels every building, and its purpose, can be identified together with the wheel pit. The furnace was the last in Wales to use charcoal and it was in operation until 1828. Another Tintern "first" came in 1760 when the original bellows was replaced by a set of blowing cylinders operated from the wheel by cranks.

10 FURNACE POND

A little further up the valley is the well preserved dam over which the road runs and a large pond for supplying the furnace. Looking downstream over the parapet, only the river now flows but the course of the leat to the furnace may still be seen at the right hand end.

11 PONT-Y-SAESON FORGE

Continuing up the road with the pond on the left, there is now a "T" junction. Turn left and on the left hand side, opposite a row of cottages, is another substantial dam though the forge pond itself is now drained out. This was the site of a very ancient forge, shown on a map of 1675. Records show that in 1695, it produced 61 tons of Osmond iron, nearly all for the Wireworks.

12 PONT-Y-SAESON UPPER WIREWORKS

Also known as New Tongs Mill, not much is accessible (and it is on private land in any case) but the site may be found by turning left again over a bridge and after a few yards a high retaining wall above the road marks the spot of the mill, fed from a leat from higher up the valley. A hard scramble up the steep bank by the wall reveals an extensive site, but it is very much overgrown.

From this point a return to the "Royal George" is suggested.

FORESTRY

The Wye Valley has some of the best areas of ancient woodland in the British Isles, some of it primeval and uncultivated to this day. The proportion of woodland to agricultural land is probably the same as it was in Roman times. Down the ages the valley has supplied timber for building and furniture, pit props and fencing, charcoal for the furnaces and oak bark for tanning. An important "export" was brushwood for strengthening the sea defences along the Severn before the building of the existing sea walls.

Since the 1920's, practically all that you can see has been managed by the Forestry Commission who have carefully maintained the appearance of the valley with mixed planting of the slower growing broad-leaf varieties, notably oak and beech, with the quick-growing conifer "cash crop" mainly confined to the upland areas. There are some fine stands of Douglas Fir and, in the spring, clouds of white wild cherry blossom appear in the sea of fresh green. The Commission also maintain well-defined and waymarked forest walks described in their leaflets obtainable from the Abbey Mill shop.

CHARCOAL

Besides providing the high temperature needed in the blast furnace, charcoal was an essential ingredient of the iron itself, supplying pure carbon to mix with the ore. Charcoal is produced by the carefully controlled slow burning of wood, methodically stacked in mounds and covered with turf to restrict the air flow. This would have been carried out in temporary camps set up in the heart of the woodland and the sites must have been numerous at the height of the industry, until the furnace closed down in 1828. Another outlet for Tintern charcoal was for the manufacture of carbon blocks for water filters, by Thos. Atkins & Co of Chepstow.

WOOD TURNING

Oak, Alder and Sycamore and other timber from the local woodlands offered a living for wood turners at both Tintern and Llandogo.

In Tintern, the turnery was the former Lower Forge (now Abbey Mill Craft Shop) where the principal products were chair legs, "stretchers" (the pieces which brace the legs), and "stumps" which support the arms. According to a local ex-employee, Mr Jim Rowlands, who died aged 93 in 1970, the average production of these was five gross per day. The working day was from six in the morning to six in the evening with half an hour for breakfast and an hour for lunch. At piecework rates which depended on the difficulty of the job, the average weekly take home pay was £1.50 in today's money. Other staple lines were rolling pins turned from a single block of sycamore, darning mushrooms, skittles, candlesticks, and at the other extreme, gross upon gross of wooden balls for coconut shies. Many of the things made were for export, taken downstream on the ubiquitous trows. The turnery finally closed down in the 1930's and became a builder's yard and carpentry.

There was another Turnery in the Trellech Road, behind Rock-leigh, run by a timber merchant, Mr Fryer, and it was here that Mr Rowlands served his apprenticeship.

BARK

Since the Middle Ages there were leather workers in all market towns and Chepstow had its full complement. The principal tanning agent was finely ground oak bark and Tintern provided a substantial share of the thousands of tons shipped down the Wye; not just for Chepstow itself, but for shipment all along the coast of Wales, across to Bristol and over to Ireland. Even before 1241, the monks at Tintern had their own tannery, but it seems they bought in their bark from some miles away - at two pence a load! Later on, they were to export it themselves.

The oak bark had to be stripped as the sap was rising, between April and the end of June. It was stripped off in two foot lengths and carefully arranged in a covered stack. Next came teams of women to clean it and to strip off any moss and the outer skin before it went to the bark house to be chopped into four inch pieces. From there, it was shipped to the merchants and tanners of Chepstow in barges carrying 20-25 tons each. There were bark yards at Tintern, and the bark house survives to this day as the "Wye Barn" Guest House right down by the river path from the Abbey behind the Anchor Hotel. The area here is known as The Quay and the barges would have been moored alongside and at the mouth of the Angidy. As the barn is within the Abbey precinct, it may even have been here where

OCCUPATIONS IN THE COMBINED PARISHES OF CHAPEL HILL AND TINTERN PARVA,

as stated in Census Returns 1841-1881

	1841	1851	1861	1871	1881
Total Population	779	782	680	746	788
Total occupied households	239	189	141	154	173
WIRE, IRON & TIN WORKS, including owners	65	99	71	38?	103
FARMING & GARDENING	18	19	15	23	30
RIVER, mariners, fishermen, watermen, ferry, shipwright and sailmaker	23	19	14	9	6
FORESTRY, woodmen, hauliers and bark cutters	20	7	7	18	18
charcoal burner		1		1	1
lime burner				1	1
BUILDING TRADES, carpenters, masons, plasterers etc.	14	22	10	13	11
CLOTHING, dressmakers/ tailors	10	13	19	8	9
cordwainers/ boot and shoe makers	12	10	8	7	4
BLACKSMITHS/ COOPERS/ HOOPSHAVERS	(1)	10	10	6	6
SHOP OWNERS & WORKERS, inc butchers, maltsters and grocers	10	8	11	9	10
LABOURERS, figures may include agricultural workers	29	29	47	46	28
INNKEEPERS/ LODGING HOUSE KEEPERS	13	8	12	9	11
DOMESTIC SERVANTS, inc charwomen and laundresses	67	24	46	61	59
GROOMS/ OSTLERS	1	3	2	3	1
KEEPER OF ABBEY		1			1
DOCTOR/ DRUGGIST	4	2	1	1	2
RECTOR/ PREACHER		2	3	1	3
TEACHER		5	3	1	3
MIDWIFE		1			
POLICEMAN			1	1	1
POSTMASTER		1	1	1	1
COAL MERCHANT					2
RAILWAY EMPLOYEES					4
TAX COLLECTOR					1
CARTER					1

N. B. Women were often employed on a part-time basis, so may not always have stated their occupation.
Some men, especially the Innkeepers, had two trades.
The 1861 Census is obviously incomplete, so it is difficult to state correct figures.

the monks stored their supply, and is close to the supposed site of the tannery.

By the latter part of the nineteenth century, however, the trade had died.

COOPERS YARD

The coopers yard was sited at the Bark Yard. The principal family involved were the Hopkins', and they made hoops, staves and barrels which were then exported. To this end, the Hopkins family actually owned some ships themselves, like the sloop "Lovely Lass", the 63 ton trow "Hornet" and the 76 ton trow "John and Mary" which was built at Brockweir in1828.

SHIP BUILDING

Unlike Brockweir, where there was a thriving ship building trade, Tintern only produced a few ships of her own. Two were registered at Chepstow, in 1788, the "Jane", an 81 ton Brig, 59'6" long and 18'4" wide, and "Industry" built in 1772, a 57 ton trow.

OTHER TRADES

In addition to the above, brief mention must be made of others:-

CORN AND OIL MILLS: besides those already mentioned, the Angidy sheltered others, but they have all disappeared. There are, however, references to one or two that were incorporated into iron works. One such reference is as far back as 1625. The firmest evidence appears in an inventory of 1821 which gives the Abbey Corn Mill one wheel and three pairs of stones.

MALTHOUSE: This was the barn-like building opposite the "Moon and Sixpence" now David Hunt's butchery and grocers shop at one end, and Tintern Garage at the other.

LIMEKILNS: These were sited behind the Beaufort Hotel, but there were others back along the Chepstow road, in the woods opposite the Livox Quarry.

BREEZE BLOCKS: These (or their fore-runners) were made at a factory by the river, on the site now occupied by the old people's bungalows, on Quayside. There would have been plenty of furnace slag available locally to make them.

LOCAL NEEDS: The many trades and occupations needed for self-sufficient community were all here too. One of the smithies was alongside the present Doctor's surgery - in a "listed" building which was demolished nevertheless; no less than four bakeries; masons, carpenters, wheelwrights, numerous shoemakers, and so on. Attached is a list of occupations, culled from the five Census from 1841-1881. One interesting job is that of Fern Gatherer, a short-lived occupation supplying to the Victorian fashion for fern gardens.

A STROLL DOWN MEMORY LANE

By Rose M Jones

When Tintern School was closed in 1985, a gathering of old pupils took place, and old photographs studied. Names of pupils from the 1920s were recalled, and then the 65 year old began to recall his early post-school years.

Leaving the village school, he went straight to work in the Forestry Commission Nursery, at Fairoak, where some 40-50 youngsters (boys and girls) were employed "lining out".

Work started at 7.00 am, and this meant, for Brian, a long early walk from Barbadoes Hill. The "boss", obviously a hard man, was there and if the hapless youngster arrived at 7.05 am, he was sent back home until 11.30 am, thereby losing half a days' pay. The youngsters were given the job of planting out young trees approximately 2"-3" high. The ground had first to be prepared meticulously - raised beds the full length of the nursery and ALL BY HAND. The trees were planted with a dibber, in long straight rows, and 2" apart, exactly. If the rules were not adhered to, the trees were taken out and the work had to be done again. The planters were divided into teams of four, each team planting a row, kneeling down. Payment was by result - 2/3 per 1,000 trees, this between four! If the weather was wet, no pay.

At 1.00 pm, a whistle was blown - time for dinner. Large tins of tea had been brewed on the open fire (a stick in each tin prevented smokey tea) and all had to get their meal. This was usually a thick slice of bread, a piece of cheese and a slice of home-cured bacon fat. The cheese was placed on a forked hazel twig and the bacon skewered onto a long one. First the cheese was toasted and put onto the bread, then the bacon, the fat dripping onto the bread and cheese. (The original barbeque!) All was now ready and with unwashed hands, the food was eaten in the "dining room" - a draughty, smokey hut.

Promptly, at 1.30 pm, the whistle blew again, and it was to kneeling down and more trees, until 4.30 pm. Then the long trek home.

A week consisted of 5½ days. If the weather was good, and all went well, it was possible for the team to earn £10 in a week. This was "good" money, as basic wages were 32/6. It must be remembered, however, that the next week could be the reverse if difficulties, rain and other snags, prevented planting. Frost, too, cut short a days work. In the Autumn, acorns had to be collected from the woods. These were put in red lead, and planted in beds covered with slats, which were hand-made in the winter.

When the trees were 1½-2 feet high, they were dug up and bundled into 50's. Many were sent to forestry sites all over the country. The rest were used locally for replanting woods which had been cleared of timber and undergrowth. Clearing of undergrowth was paid for at the rate of 2/3 per chain (22 yards). For local use, the bundles of trees were often left at the Saw Mills in the village, to be picked up by the workers who had to carry their own supply to the place of work - often quite a distance. A satchel was provided.

Our friend then recalled working with Jack Charles when all the timber in Coed Beddick was cut. The steep slope of the land made it too difficult to work horses. Mr John Jones (Saw Mills) had an old traction engine in his shed, unused for years. They got permission to clean it up, and found it worked! Jack Charles drove it up to the wood, and as they went up the Trellech Road, he let his companion drive. Even to this day, the thrill of that achievement was obvious! Getting the engine started had its drawbacks too! It meant a 5.00 am start, to get steam up, ready for the men to start work at 7.00 am. Later, when all was cleared, he helped to plant the wood with young trees - oak and beech. Why not go up and see them?

Is it any wonder this boy has become the best gardener in the village. His small garden, planted in neat, straight rows of vegetables, without a weed, every inch utilized, and super quality. Flowers, too, and in the cupboard, cups, shields and diplomas for his efforts. No doubt he learned at an early age that from those tiny acorns, neatly sown, grew the mighty oak!

N.B. He still rises early in the morning!

A May Evening

Who would be in city streets
On such a night as this
The river dreaming through the valley,
Oh such gentle bliss!

To sit upon its warm green banks
The air so fresh and clean,
As pale translucent dusk descends
And night creeps in unseen.

The sun that burned so hot all day
Has kissed the land and gone,
But though the twilight hints of chill
Her warm breath lingers on.

And high above the shadowed woods,
A pale young moon takes flight,
And all around the air is filled
With muted sounds of night.

Oh who indeed could be in town
On such a night in May
For if there be a heav'n on earth
"This here - at close of day.

June M Hodges

Elver Fishing

When the high-tides co-incide with late evening, during the month of April, the banks of the River Wye come alive with the lamps of the elver fishermen. Witnesses can see an event that has occurred here since time immemorial, when local families, armed with their nets, not unlike those used for lacrosse!, line the banks to scoop out the millions of wriggling baby eels, no bigger than matchsticks, known as elvers. Consumed with relish by the "locals", elvers now command high prices and when grown to eels they are much prized in the Far East.

The elvers are thoroughly washed, boiled and strained. They are then pressed into "cheeses". Thick slices are cut, and fried with bacon, and are considered a great delicacy.

TINTERN ON THE WYE

By Elaine Dollery

Two Hundred years ago, the Wye,
Was full of trows, all passing by
Or loading cargoes, here and there
At Chepstow, Tintern or Brockweir.

The quays were piled with wood and coal,
And shipmen made the barrels roll.
The excise man, with anxious care
Would tax the wine tuns lying there.

The abbey trows would stack their wool,
The malt house stores were often full,
And with the tide, its ebbs and flows,
Would sail, like swans, the bustling trows.

Tintern has two main facets, the Wye and the Abbey, and these two have formed its history. Early settlements, abbeys and monasteries, were usually on the banks of rivers, so that flocks could be watered, crops grown, fish eaten, and people and goods could be transported.

Formerly the river was a vital highway for cargoes, and a thoroughfare for sightseers. Nowadays we have a few canoeists; fishermen after trout, salmon or elvers; and we have tourists, who come to share the beauty of the valley. On Easter Monday there is a Duck Race, when yellow plastic ducks with lottery numbers on their tummies, are emptied by the sack load into the Wye at Brockweir and float down to Tintern, cheered on enthusiastically by those who have bought a duck for the day.

Because the Wye is tidal, and Tintern stands on the edge of it, there have always been floods. A normal tide is up to 10 or 11 feet, but at the equinox, that is when day and night are equal in length in Spring and Autumn (about 21st March, 23rd September) tides can rise to 18 feet. Abnormal rainfall (as has happened this February 1990,) when the water pours in torrents off the hills, plus the normal flux and fall caused by the moon, and you will realise why many Tintern doorsteps are regularly covered in sandbags.

The Church of St Michael floods occasionally. When the river is high, the carpets are taken up, and the water seeps in through the floor of the old porch, and laps gently at the edge of the raised pews. There are photographs in the church of the time it rose as high as the chancel, and as a precaution all the electrics have been raised above flood level.

Where there is a river, there are tragedies, and one of the "Tragical Events" connected with Tintern occurred on 20th September, 1812. Two families staying at the Beaufort Arms in Chepstow hired 2 post chaises to take them to a service in Tintern. As it was a fair day, they hired a pleasure boat to return on the evening tide to their hostelry. Alas, the ebb tide was running very strongly, and a rope from a brig near Chepstow Bridge caught and overturned the boat and 7 out of the 12 passengers drowned. These included 6 ladies, one elderly, but most "in the flower of their youth and beauty" and an attendant footman. In the pocket book belonging to the lady was found morning text for the service:- "For to me to live is Christ, and to die is gain", and on the opposite page was the sketch she had made earlier that day of Tintern Abbey.

Because of tides and currents, Chepstow bridge has always been a navigational hazard to shipping: for example on 19th May, 1863, a small barge belonging to a Mr Good of Brockweir was towing a larger one to which between 25 and 30 tons of oak timber had been lashed to form a raft. She struck the centre pier at low tide and settled down on the mud, to be refloated next day as the tide rose. It is also recorded that on 3rd December 1785 the "Abbey" trow belonging to Pritchard of Tintern, ran aground at the rivers mouth with a cargo of grain; and in January 1873 the "Richard" laden with stone for Bristol, settled down on the bank under Tintern church and filled with water as the tide turned. It was later refloated to continue its journey downstream. St Michael's must be one of the few churches to have had a shipwreck at the edge of its churchyard!

Trows often settled on the mud awaiting the tide and many trowmen would take advantage of these occasions by wading ashore, and raiding swedes or anything portable from the nearby farms. Trowmen and their vessels were an important part of river life, and the men were protected by law from the press gangs until 1798, unlike less favoured mariners, who were regularly shipped off unwillingly to serve in the King's Navy.

In the eleventh century the Vikings swept up the rivers Severn, Wye and Usk, and the original trows were a modification of a Viking craft. Strong wooden sailing vessels that could lie mud bound without harm, and yet be light enought to ride the bore, trows were undecked sloops characteristic of both the Severn and Wye up to the beginning of the twentieth century.

Many and varied cargoes travelled the river in trows, and the

Wye was a busy waterway. From 1693 on, copper from Redbrook was exported to Chepstow. Charcoal was brought from Tintern to Chepstow for the manufacture of carbon blocks for water filters at Thomas Atkins & Co in St Anne's Lane. Coal and iron ore, provisions and firewood, went from the Wye Valley to towns nearby, and the Abbot of Tintern had a vessel which regularly traded with Bristol.

There were quarries in the area from very early times, and in the nineteenth century the trows carried limestone to make the docks at Sharpness, Avonmouth, and Newport, and to strengthen sea walls in the Severn estuary. Later, loads were carried by strings of barges towed by steam tugs, but the workhorse of the Wye was the trow.

The Wye was navigable as far up as Hereford until 1845, and timber and bark would be sent downstream after heavy rain or on spring tides. On a good flood tide, Severn trows could travel from Lydney to Gloucester in two hours, and at one time there were thirty to forty trows on the Wye.

These trows came from Chepstow, Tintern, Brockweir, Redbrook and Llandogo, and the masts of the larger vessels could be lowered to pass beneath Chepstow bridge. Only two are known to have been built at Tintern, but these give us an idea of the size of the cargoes. First was the "Industry" registered in 1772, and again in 1789; she was a single masted trow of 57 tons, 52'10" long, and 16' 4" in breadth, with a draught of 5'2". Owned by Edward Madley of Llandogo, she was "lost on English Stones May 29th, 1804". The second was the "Jane", registered in 1788, a brig of 81 tons, 59'6" long, and 18'4" in width. Her master was one Mark MacDonald, and the owner, Thomas Davis, was a merchant of Abbey Tintern.

Although many smaller trows of about 12 tons were built at Monmouth, Redbrook and Llandogo, in the late eighteenth century some boats were built up to 100 tons. The "Hopewell" of 1810 was 120 tons, and the "Wye", which was launched at Brockweir in 1848, was up to 156 tons. The larger trows would navigate as far as Brockweir, and then unload their cargoes into smaller craft, which would continue upstream. Nowadays the river is navigable only as far as Brockweir, and although one man managed to sail a large boat to Hereford recently by making use of the high tides, it took him a long time, and he nearly got stuck under Monmouth bridge.

To realise how important the river traffic was to the valleys, you have only to keep your eyes open as you travel. If you visit the church of St Oudoceus in Llandogo, you can see the Bell of the

"William and Sarah" above the south door. In Bristol an inn called "Landoger Trow" was used as Long John Silver's "spy-glass" in Treasure Island, and there are numerous relics of the boats along the banks of the Wye, either as artifacts, or in place names such as "Fisherman's Wharf", or "Quay House", which was the home of the former Quaymaster.

Besides the trows, there were ferries and coracles. Within living memory a ferry used to run from the Anchor Inn to Brockweir. It took half an hour and cost a sixpenny fare. There was also a regular Sunday boat trip after church from Tintern to Brockweir, as in pre referendum days, Tintern, being a godly place was dry, while Brockweir was blessed with three pubs. This outing was a great favourite.

Coracles on the other hand were small, and usually built for one man only. Once a common sight on the Wye, they looked like battered bath tubs made of interwoven willow twigs and covered in horse hide. Designed to be carried on the fisherman's back, they were flat bottomed, about five foot long, and propelled by a single oar. Although very hard to manoeuvre, as they had a tendency to spin in circles, many fishermen were adepts, and "an adventurous fellow, for a wager, once navigated a coracle as far as the Isle of Lundy, at the mouth of the Bristol Channel from Ross, but it did take him a full two weeks.

The people of Tintern have always been connected with the Wye, and an 1841 survey of the population of Tintern Parva and Chapel Hill showed how many of the 334 males employed in the two villages were directly involved with the river. Tintern Parva had an Excise Officer, who no doubt dealt not only with passing cargoes, but also exports of the local cider. It is known that the Abbey monks tended a vineyard somewhere in Tintern, and vines have been recently replanted on the slopes above the Wye Valley Hotel, which are again producing some interesting and prize winning local wines.

These days you need a permit to fish on the Wye, and various clubs, groups or landowners own certain stretches of water, or pitches. The Cistercians of Tintern Abbey were notoriously greedy over the expansion of their fishing rights, which were a jealously guarded source of food and income. A survey of the manor of Trellech, made 19th October, 1677, states that:-

"The Reeve collects the homage rents, the fishery belongs to the Lord; but Henry Probert, Esq of Pantyglase, son and heir to Sir George Probert, Knight, deceased, hath a right of fishing from a certain crab tree growing upon the English shore of the River Wye between Brockware and Lynware, and from

there to a certain stone below Tintarne Church called Lawrence Bead, which said stone devideth the fishing of the said earle and the said Marquis of Worcester. Tenants bordering on the Wye have the right of fishing with angles and wheels over against their own lands and gravels".

Another way of catching fish was by the use of weirs: these were either dams across the river, or "a fence of stakes set in a stream for catching fish". The word comes from the old English word "wer", meaning an enclosed trap.

The four main weirs were:- Plum weir, Ash weir, Ithels weir and Wal weir, but originally there were many more. In the Charter of William, Earl Mareschall, to Tintern Abbey, on 22nd March 1223, the weirs between Brockweir and Chepstow are named as:

Brockwear, Linwear, Aswere (Ash weir), Plumwear, Astandwere (Stow weir), and Wals wear, near a large oak tree; Badwingwere, opposite a cliff of the same name; Halfwear, opposite the troughs for supplying Livox Farm with water, and Wayfhere, a pool opposite Lancaut. Ashwere was in existence in the 14th century, and was supposedly pulled down in the late 1600s. In 1958, a Mr D Edwards examined the site and noticed several large stone blocks were visible in the bed of the river, with others embedded in the bank. The broken surface of the otherwise smooth flowing river indicated that remains of the weir still existed below the surface. Lynn Weir, also mentioned in 1223, was pulled down after 1695. Fishing at the weir is mentioned in documents in the 14th century, and in one, dated 1409-10, it mentions the destruction of the fishery, and it has been suggested that this could be linked with the Owen Glyndwr's raid in the area in 1404. After being rebuilt this was later destroyed by floods.

The Wye is famous for salmon fishing, and these days salmon poachers have taken up to 30 fish in one night. Apart from the illegality, this results in overfishing and damage to fish stocks, and the same is happening with the elvers.

Various methods have been used to harvest the fish, and in 1823, Charles Heath wrote a vivid description:- "Salmon Fishing, in the Wye, which is from the middle of November to the middle of August employs a number of people. The method used for taking them is, by mooring a boat (one end near the shore) with a net fixed to two poles:- upon the fish striking against the net, the men press down the poles, which raises up the net, and secures the salmon.

This is a business of great uncertainty; but when fortunate, well rewards the PATIENT fishermans' ANXIOUS toil. They are often out more then twelve hours at a time, the greater part of which is in the night".

This of course would be an anathema to the serious salmon fisherman, who can be seen peacefully sitting by the banks of the Wye with his rods, while the stately swans float serenely by. Trout are numerous also, but the fish that causes the most competition is probably the humble eel. With their snake like bodies, 260 vertebrae, and weighing up to 15 lbs or more, these can travel long distances overland, which explains why they are sometimes found in isolated waters. They spawn in special groups in the Sargasso sea, at a depth of some 7,000 metres, and some ten per cent die after spawning from exhaustion.

After a period of years the fry return to European rivers, helped by the Atlantic drift. For protection, these form themselves into wriggling writhing fish balls of up to 3 cwt, and roll up to the estuary, where they then divide, and continue upstream. Shoals of young eels or elvers come upstream in May, and the spawning tides are in November and December. There is great competition over territorial rights at this time and considerable overfishing. There is a holding tank in Brockweir to contain the catch, and these elvers are then exported to Japan. The Japanese have an enormous appetite for fish, and provide an inexhaustible market, so the successful fisherman can earn considerable sums.

The Wye has always been vital to Tintern: its fords and weirs, mariners and fishermen formed a way of life dependent on the river. The trows were its life blood, ferrying cargoes to places far and near, and spreading out from the Wye Valley into the world outside, and even now people come to see the beauty that remains.

TINTERNS' PIRATE

One of Tinterns' more notorious sons was John Callice. Born some time before the middle of the sixteenth century at Tintern, he left at the age of twelve for London. There, he joined the household of Alderman Bond and trained to be a merchant. No doubt, he was well acquainted with ships and sailing from his childhood by a river, so he soon adapted to a life of a trader. However, he soon became bored with legitimate seafaring, and by 1571, Callice had embarked on a career of piracy. Successful as a pirate, he was often at loggerheads with the Courts! He seemed to lead a charmed life, frequently avoiding punishment even though the Queen threatened to deport him! No doubt he had friends in high places. His father-in-law was William Herbert of Cardiff believed to be a kinsman of the Earl of Pembroke, and John Callice seems to have maintained his links with Tintern, claiming his mothers' estates, as heir, in 1577. He died about 1587/8, supposedly in Barbary.

The Parish Records of both Chapel Hill and Tintern Parva only go back as far as the turn of the seventeenth century, but it is interesting to note that a baptism of Mary, daughter of Richard and Mary Calys in 1696 is recorded.

◆ ◆ ◆ ◆

The Day Book of Thomas Ansley, the Quay Master of Brockweir, notes that on January 29th, 1846, the Wye experienced the highest tide that had been known for many years, with one thousand sheep and several horses lost in different places. The River Usk obviously experienced the same, as "The Monmouthshire Merlin" for the 31 January, 1846 writes that the high tide was "unprecedented in the memory of the most aged inhabitant" of Usk town.

TINTERNS' CHURCHES

By Adrian Smith

Apart from the glorious ruins of the Cistercian Abbey of St Mary, Tintern boasts three "live" churches - Riverside Methodist Chapel, the Pentecostal Chapel, and the parish church of St Michael and All Angels - and the ruins of St Marys' Church, Chapel Hill. Also of interest is the former Bible Christians' Chapel in the lower Angidy Valley, now Chapel Garage.

The ruined *St Marys' Church*, at Chapel Hill, (also referred to as Abbey Tintern, or Abaty Tyndyrn), stands on Chapel Hill below the eastern end of Glyn Woods, and above the Beaufort Hotel. The spectacular view of the twin villages - Abbey Tintern and Tintern

Parva - and of the Abbey itself is a worthwhile reward for the steep climb up the cobbled path, lined with blackthorn from which many bottles of sloe gin have been made.

The church, which was rebuilt in 1866, stands on the site of a medieval chapel, probably built as a retreat for the monks of the Abbey Church, or for the secular community growing outside the Abbey walls. Parish records date back to 1695, and reflect the more populous and hectic days of the Angidy Valley's industrial period. The earliest monumental inscription is in memory of Francis Bradford, dated 1657, who founded the Bradford Charity. The church formerly contained a rood screen, a wooden pulpit and a sanctuary chair, all the work of William Jones who was parish clerk in the 1890s.

St Mary's Church is mentioned in the work by Bradney, Monmouthshire, where the incumbents are listed from 1717. It was at various times associated with the parishes of Llandogo, Trellech, Llanishen as well as Tintern Parva, being finally annexed to the latter in 1902. The Church became redundant in 1972, and some of the contents were sold to Clearwell Castle. The Communion Plate, altar cross, processional cross and candlesticks are to be found in St Michaels' Church. St Marys' was destroyed by fire in July 1977.

The graveyard contains several interesting monuments including one to Peter Carr who died 14 October 1913 in the Senghenydd Pit disaster, and a war grave to Private P. B. Hall, an American citizen who enlisted in the Lancashire Fusiliers, and who died at Connaught Hospital, Farnborough, 5 March, 1919 at the age of 22. The yard is still in use to this day.

The parish church of *St Michael and All Angels* lies at the northern end of Tintern Parva, or, in Welsh, Llanfihangel Tyndyrn, on the banks of the River Wye (Afon Gwy). Arguably, it is the nearest church within the Anglican Province of Wales to the Anglican Province of England as the border runs mid-river, some one hundred yards away. It stands on an ancient site - the excellent book, "Fedw Villages" by Raymond Howells, refers to a Celtic establishment there in 765 AD. The medieval "Liber Llandaffiensis" mentions that St Tewdrig "retired" to a hermits' cell at Tintern in 555AD.

Bradney lists the incumbents from 1348, the patron being the Crown until the seventeenth century. Thereafter, patronage passed to the Lords of Tintern Manor, including William Fielding, Thomas Fielding and John Curre of Itton.

The present church was rebuilt in 1846. An ancient picture of the previous building shows it to be much as it is today but lacking the nave extension to the west of the medieval porch. The sanctuary contains an aumbry and the Priests' Door into the Chancel, which was closed at that time, can still be discerned. The south porch has a fine groined vaulted roof, with Tudor roses, with an empty niche over the exterior of the door. The windows in the north wall of the nave appear to be much older than those in the south, leading one to believe that they may have been retained from the old church.

In the aisle is a memorial to Elizabeth Feilding, wife of William, died January 1703, as well as some ancient, broken tombstones, probably brought from the yard during the 1846 restoration. Of these, one is dated 1668, whilst another has the outline of a two-handled broad-sword, some five feet long, no doubt commemmorating a medieval knight. Memorials in the church include that to Herbert Hilary, son of Caleb and Rose Coy of Tintern, who came to enlist in the 1st Welch Regiment from New York, and fell at Ypres on the 25th May 1919, aged 19. John Roberts, a former maltster, merchant and ship owner, died 1875 aged 70, his wife Julia, and his five sons are also commemorated. The reading lamps in the pulpit and on the Rector's stall, the stall itself and the lectern all bear dedications, the lectern being in memory of the four Tintern men who fell in the 2nd World War. The east window is dedicated to Jane Damaris Audland, wife of the surgeon John Audland. The oak chair in the Chancel is made from the old oak roof timbers of the medieval roof.

The church registers date from 1756 (marriages) and 1812 (baptisms and burials). The church yard contains several ancient tombs, dating back to 1620. Samuel Small and his wife lie adjacent to the east side of the sanctuary wall; he died in April 1623 - and was clearly well named! Also of interest are the nearby tombs of members of the Luff family - to this day a village name. The two gates to the yard both bear interesting dedications.

TINTERN'S CHARITIES

By Rose M Jones

Chapel Hill United Charities

Many senior citizens in Tintern wonder how they come to receive, each December, a gift, under the heading of "Chapel Hill United Charities".

Tintern Manor House, now demolished. Taken from Bradney's "Monmouthshire", from a painting by M. E. Bagnall-Oakley

Tintern Station

View of The Quay, showing Quay Cottages, Quay House and The Bark House. Notice the Trow in the foreground.

"ABBY TINTERN" before the Car Park!

Interior of St Mary's Church , since destroyed by fire.

The Angidy Valley, earlier this century

The Royal George Hotel, as it once was

Opening day of the Abbey Stores.

SKETCH MAP OF TINTERN

showing the old parishes of Chapel Hill & Tintern Parva, & principle landmarks.

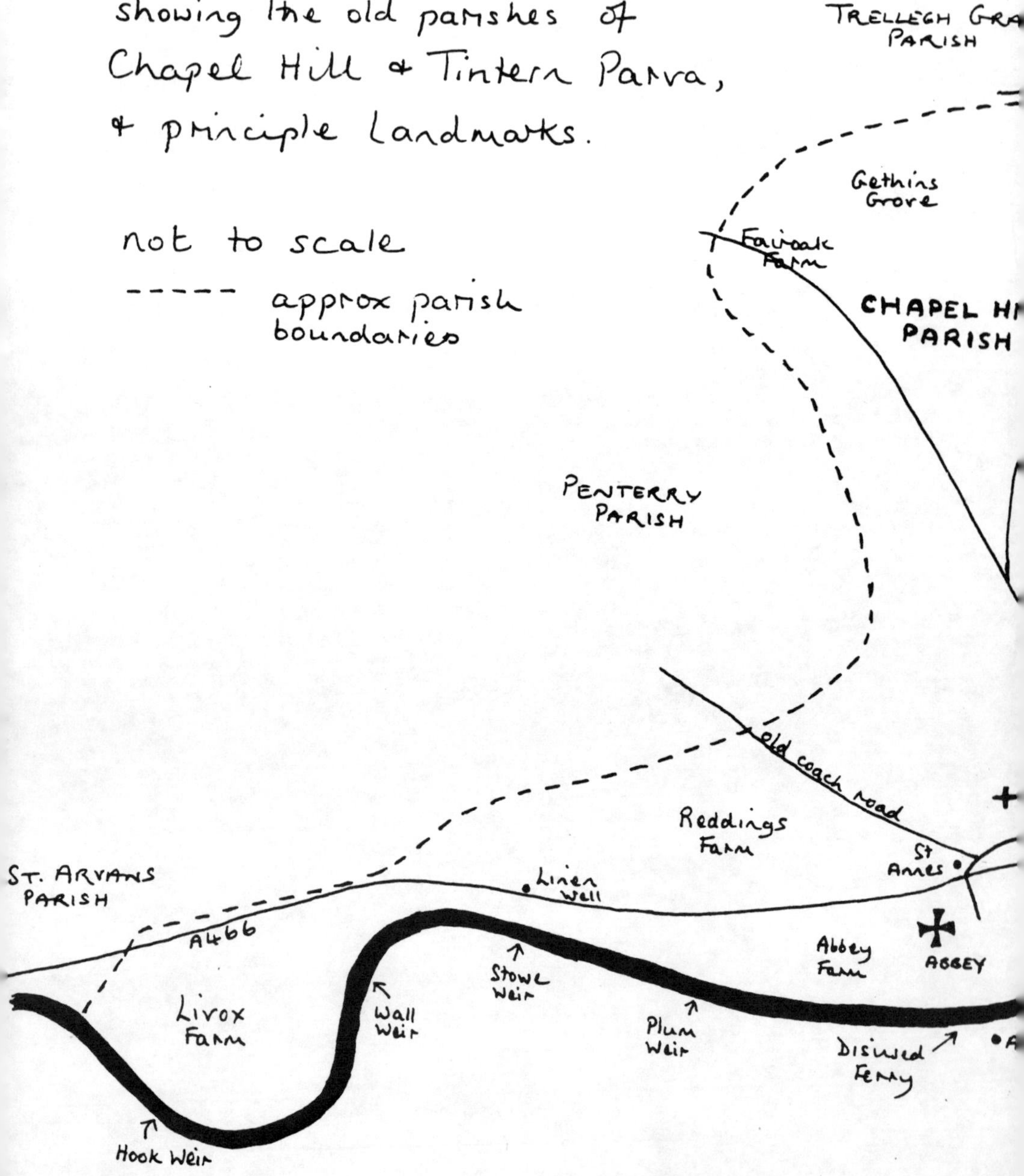

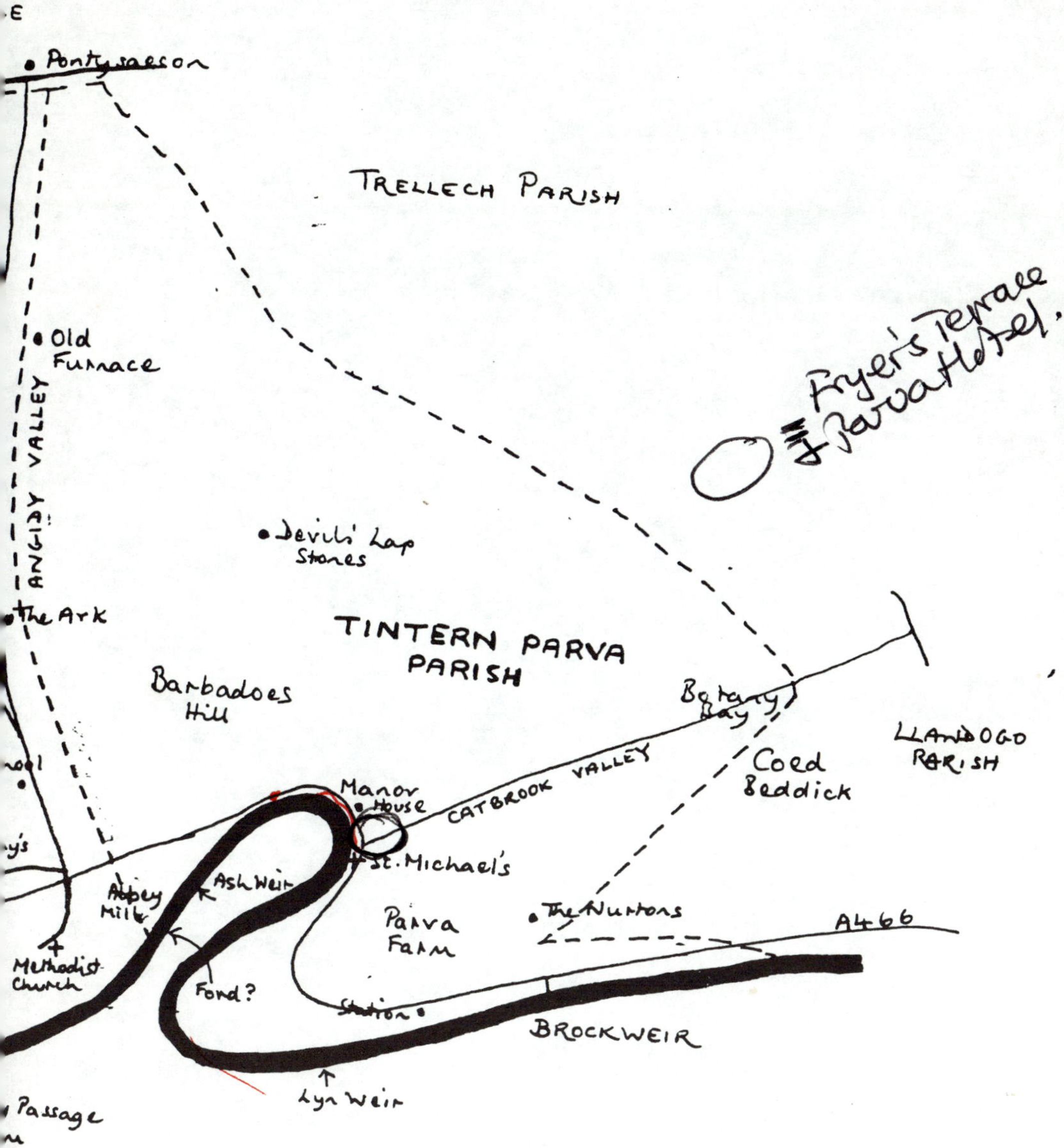

Pontysaeson
TRELLECH PARISH
Old Furnace
ANGIDY VALLEY
Devils' Lap Stones
The Ark
TINTERN PARVA PARISH
Barbadoes Hill
Botany Bay
LLANDOGO PARISH
Coed Beddick
Manor House
CATBROOK VALLEY
St. Michael's
Ash Weir
Abbey Mill
The Nurtons
A466
Parva Farm
Methodist Church
Ford?
Station
BROCKWEIR
Lyn Weir
Passage

View of Tintern, with Ashweir House and the Rose and Crown on the left.

One hundred years later - Sadlers (now the tearoom) Ashweir House & The Rose and Crown

TINTERN PARVA CHURCH. (From a drawing made shortly before the rebuilding in 1846.)

View of St Michael's Church, prior to rebuilding in 1846, taken from Bradneys' "Monmouthshire".

St Michaels' showing the wharf

Pre-War British Legion Fete, on "The Leytons". Capt Sharp, of the Beaufort, on the right, with hat and stick.

"Dad's Army" - The Home Guard, photographed in the Abbey, during the 2nd World War.

Tinterns' Football Team in the Early 50's

Tintern Abbey, The Anchor and The Slipway

This scheme, devised for the regulation of Charities, was drawn up in 1910, and is controlled by the Charity Commissioners. There are five Trustees. The Rector is an ex-officio member and acts as Chairman, and the other four are elected by the Community Council, but are not necessarily serving members. A non-member is secretary.

1 Philip and Thomas Hackett - Indenture dated 10th December 1634 - for the benefit of the Poor in the Ancient Parishes of Chapel Hill and Tintern Parva, today combined into the modern parish of Tintern. This comprises approximately twelve acres of land at Mounton, known as Monck Redding. At present, as this land is within the Green Belt, it would not be possible to get building permission, so it is rented out to a local farmer.

2 Samuel Prichard - Decree of High Court, 14 November 1818. This too, is for the benefit of the poor, of the two parishes. This is a sum of £625-5s-6d, invested in Consols by the Charity Commissioners. The Pritchards were an old Chapel Hill family, and his will is dated 27 December, 1810.

3 The Poor's Field - Foundation before 1833. The charity for this was the income from approximately four acres at Penterry, and was sold for £70 in 1966. This is now invested by the Charity Commissioners.

The income from these three charities is distributed annually in December, to everyone over the age of 65, without regard to position etcetera, in a voucher form that has to be spent with the local trades-people.

The Bradford Charity

The Bradford Charity is administered by the same Trustees as the Chapel Hill United Charities. The income was to pay for the apprenticing of a poor boy, resident in Chapel Hill to a useful trade or occupation. If there was no applicant, then the income went to a similarly placed boy in Tintern Parva. This application has, today, also altered, and now a grant, subject to the availability of funds, is normally paid to a boy or girl who is learning a profession or trade, and helps pay for tools or books.

This Charity was founded by the Will of Francis Bradford, dated 18 June, 1656, and proved in the Prerogative Court of Canterbury in 1657. It comprises a "rent charge from an estate of 60 acres at Llangattock Juxta, Usk, in the county of Monmouth". In 1974, the owners of this estate, Upper Court Farm, sold up, and the new owners applied to redeem the rent charge. This was allowed, and as a result £200 was invested by the Commisioners in Charities Offficial Investment Fund Income Shares.

Francis Bradford had been clerk of the Wire Works, and was brother of William Bradford of Bristol. His wife, Anne, was the daughter of Richard Bond of Redbrook and sister of George Bond of Wyeseal. After Francis died, Anne married Henry Thomas, who died in 1661, and then she married for a third time, Roger Allde of Hardwick.

Charles Heath, of Monmouth, quotes from the diary of John Gwynne, one time resident of Chapel Hill:

> *"Francis Bradford died on Thursday 1 October 1657 by a fall from his horse going to Whitebrook, falling headlong in a swoon forward upon the horse's neck, with his two feet in the stirrups, his wife was with him, and she present alighted of her horse and cried for help, soe he was carried down in a trow to Abby, and was sick for about a week, burried on the Saturday following*".

A SUNDAY SCHOOL OUTING

By Sid Jones

The year is 1915. At last the day we were impatiently waiting for had arrived. The sun was shining, and it was just 9.00 o'clock. The occasion, our "outing" to Beachley for the Methodist Sunday School Children.

We assembled at the "Cross". No-one was late. Our transport was ready - a farm wagon with seats on each side and drawn by two heavy horses. Both had been beautifully groomed, their well-polished harness gleaming in the sunshine. We, too, had been well cleaned and *so* tidy!

As I recall, the ostlers were Jim Simmonds and George Sadler, and the children were in the care of Lucy Waite and helpers.

Very soon we were on our way. No 30 miles per hour speed limit, just a gentle 4 miles an hour. The journey took about 2½ hours, but with much singing and endless talking there were no complaints. At last we reached the end of the road, Beachley Pier.

We got off quickly and made a dash for the little sweet shop to spend some of our coppers. Then we all made our way to the "Point"overlooking the lighthouse. The tide was bank high and the older boys and girls soon changed into swimming clothes and were in the water. This was brown in colour and well-laced with Severn mud! No concern about pollution in those days!

By the time all were out again and dry, the grown-ups with the party had carried baskets of goodies and drinks from the road and spread it all out on the tablecloths on the grass. What a sight it was - we soon made short work of it, putting everything out of sight.

The rest of the day was spent playing games - cricket and rounders - with frequent journeys back to the sweet shop. Later in the afternoon more food appeared, and this was treated in the same way as the first meal.

Time was now running out as we made our way back to the "Pier" where the horses, well fed and watered, were hitched up ready for our homeward journey. Taking our seats, tired but happy and not quite so clean, with a last dash to the shop for the lucky ones, we were on our way, to the cheers of the locals and onlookers.

Sadly, we arrived back in Tintern one short. When we got to Golden Hill, one of the girls decided the load was too heavy for the horses to pull up the hill, so she opted to walk to ease the burden. As she walked, John Watkins from the Mason's Arms (Moon and Sixpence) came along in his car - an Overland (AX8). He picked Dolly up, and she arrived back home in state! So you see, kindness to our dumb friends does pay off!

TINTERN AND THE ARTS

By Elaine Dollery

Masefield wrote:

"One road leads to London. One road leads to Wales".

and the Welsh borders, with its castles and cliffs, church buildings and beautiful scenery, has always been a source of inspiration to poets, artists, and writers.

Religion and literature go hand in hand. Early poems, recited orally round the fireside in the long winter evenings, were handed down from father to son, growing and changing as the stories were told and retold by successive generations.

The early Silurians had a warrior god called Ocelus, dabbled in water worship, and had a cat cult. The Romans had a motley assortment of gods and goddesses; while the Saxons worshipped Woden, a native version of the Norse Odin, and named a day of the week Wednesday in his honour. The oral tradition glorified war, and told of historical events, myths and rhyming riddles, and the line between alliterative prose and poetry was indistinguishable.

It was not until the establishment of the monastic tradition that some of these stories were written down. Pagan gods would become replaced by Christian beliefs, for few people outside the Church could read or write, and books were rare and valuable. The monks in their cloisters painstakingly copied books by hand, and religious texts were inscribed, with their borders embellished with miniature paintings or devils, angels, leaves and flowers. Here the line between art and writing was indistinguishable. Next came legal documents, land titles and historical texts, and so in this way Tintern Abbey would have been involved in the early literature of the time.

The oral vernacular tradition, and the written Latin texts were supplemented by the travelling minstrels of the middle ages. These were not only entertainers, but newsbringers, and formed part of an international brotherhood of storytellers. Poets and artists have always travelled, and the valley of Tintern with its Abbey and scenery was at its most popular in the eighteenth and nineteenth centuries.

There are many references to the Wye Valley, and it is said that Henry Fielding (1707-54) wrote "Tom Jones" at Tintern in a Tudor Mansion then known as Abbots House. Although this was reputedly attacked and ruined by roundheads in the civil war, the present manor house still stands on the same site. In 1911, an eccentric American called Dr Orville Owen, excavated the bed of the Wye river near Chepstow, looking for Manuscripts to prove that Francis Bacon wrote Shakespeare's plays; and among others many of the Romantic poets mention the valley in their poems.

Coleridge for instance describes the Wyndcliff as "The whole world imaged in its vast circumference", and we know that Thomas Gray, Turner and Wordsworth all went on the Wye Valley Tour, with its spectacular views. This had various vantage points: a lovers' leap, a grotto, a Druids Temple and a giant's cave complete with guardian giant, at Piercefield now crumbled away. Southey came also, and on 13 July 1798, Wordsworth "a worshipper of Nature", came with his sister Dorothy down the Wye in a trow, and he wrote his "Lines composed a Few Miles Above Tintern Abbey".

The Gothic horror novels flourished at the same time as the Romantics. Both were inspired by wild and beautiful countryside, but whereas Mrs Radcliffe wrote of mournful haunted castles, and ghosts howling in the wind of ruined abbeys, the poets would write of the fairer, happier aspects of nature. Jane Austen wrote her novel "Northanger Abbey" as a burlesque on the horror novels, and in it a young girl, Catherine Morland, fed on an undiluted diet of penny dreadfuls from the Lending Library, falls in love with a young man, whose peppery papa, General Tilney lives in an abbey. She of course suspects the General of murdering his defunct wife, and the whole book is a gentle debunking of her gothic imagination. Tintern Abbey in its ivied ruined state provided inspiration for both Gothic and romantic literature.

The Arthurian legends are also connected with Wales. The original tales were a wonderful mixture of history, fantasy and mythology and these inspired a whole range of books, from the "Morte D'Arthur" of Malory to Tennyson's "Idylls of the King".

The grave of Arthur has been placed both at Tintern Abbey, and at Glastonbury, and Tennyson wrote of

Sir Pelleas of the isles . . . . .
Riding at noon, a day or twain before,
Across the forest called of Dean, to find
Caerleon and the King",

and again in his poem "In Memoriam",

"*There twice a day the Severn fills;*
The salt sea water passes by,
And hushes half the babbling Wye
And makes a silence in the hills.

Tintern also had its local writers. Edward Davies, who lived in Chepstow, in his poem "Chepstow - A Poem" describes the Tintern Wireworks:

"*Black Forges smoke, and noisy hammers beat,*
Where sooty Cyclops, puffing, drink and sweat;
Confront the curling flames, nor back retire,
But live, like salamanders, in the fire".

and John Loraine Baldwin, who died at St Anne's in Tintern on 25 November 1896, wrote a book called "Laws of Short Whist". He was a cricketer and Warden of Tintern Abbey, and an authority on

West End club rules, and card games. No doubt he would be delighted that the village still has a regular whist night!

Of the many artists who have visited the valley, the most famous of the Romantic school of landscape artists was of course William Turner, who painted delicate water colours of the Abbey interior, with its Gothic architecture and dramatic background. In 1782, The Reverend William Gilpin published a guidebook for the Wye tour, and he was more fascinated by the setting of the Abbey, the woods, the enfolding hills, and its air of timeless peace. However he considered the gable ends a vulgarity, and advised the remedial use of "a mallet judiciously used", although he did have the grace to add that no-one would dare to do so! He was vicar of Boldre from 1777 and a keen educationist. He is remembered as the protagonist of "the picturesque", establishing precise rules for the production of this effect in his essays.

There have been many local artists. More recently, Joseph John Alsop, a famous portrait and landscape painter, who first exhibited in the Royal Academy at the age of 23, lived at Chepstow and Tutshill. He died in 1954 aged 87, and his ashes were scattered in the Wye he loved so much. Ivor and Mercedes Waters of Chepstow have written many beautifully illustrated local books which make fascinating reading, and Donald Henry Floyd lived in Tintern after the Great War. Born in 1892, he served in Palestine, remaining a private on principle during his service, and he was a regular exhibitor at the Royal Academy.

Finally we must not forget the more modern artists, who work not with paints and canvas, but capture art on film with a camera. At present we have three well known local photgraphers, whose work is well known from publications and exhibitions: Keith Arnatt, Sue Packer, and David Hurn. But perhaps the greatest influence for the arts that Tintern now has, is in the visitors who come to see our Abbey, river, historical buildings, and enfolding hills, and take away with them photographs of a pleasant day spent in the beautiful surroundings, which have inspired so many poets and artists of the past.

◆ ◆ ◆ ◆

Extract from " A poem on The Wye Valley from Chepstow to Ross" by F Morgan, of Whitelye, Tintern published before the last war.

The sun it was shining one beautiful day
As I looked on the Abbey while the lambs were at play,
I thought of the men who had built in the past,
And still the old Abbey is standing up fast.

When you look at the Abbey and there see its mounds
You can think of the founder that lies in its grounds;
I never did see him - I wasn't there -
But they tell me his name it was Gilbert de Clare.

He must have been taken to - him and his Queen -
When Oliver Cromwell came on the scene;
He fixed up his cannons they say on Turk's ground
And some of the Abbey it soon tumbled down.

In days that are past they must have been right
To build up high windows to let in the light.
When first it was built it must have been good -
For nearly nine hundred long years it has stood.

There are people from London that come all the way
To see the old Abbey and, of course, they do pay,
It goes to the Crown, they say its their right -
To see it by day or on moonlight night.

You never see people and can say they are shabby
Who come in their cars to look round the Abbey.
Some come by the roads and some by the line,
And all these good people are dressed up so fine.

There's a place by the Abbey they call Abbey Farm
Where you get pure milk - it will do you no harm,
They sell it by day and sell it by night -
You take it from me that the milk's real white.

It comes from the cattle that are fed on good land,
And the owner being noted for leading a band;
He seems like a man who has got to the fore
For he buys up the cattle and sheep by the score.

There's a man near the Abbey with daughter and sons,
He sends off the pit-wood in trucks by the tons,
But if you want milk this he will provide
For he has a herd on the Gloucester side.

They cut up the timber right down to small pegs
And a lot whirls around and comes out chair legs.
If you do want timber for window or sills
You can get all supplied at the Lower Sawmills.

When going round the Abbey, if weather is cold,
Go into the Anchor, I believe it will hold
You, then get a warm and ask for some gin -
If good you can ask all your friends to come in.

If you ask for some things and they cannot be found
There's a place just above on a bit higher ground;
You can play the piano and sing and make charms
You can get all you need at the old Beaufort Arms.

There are things interesting right up to Old Forge
But I must keep down on the cross by the George
Or poem will lengthen and get very wide;
I'll just have the room to put in the pool side.

In walking to Tintern I pass Rose and Crown
The Mason's is busy but the Carpenter's hit down;
It was not a man who was driving a car,
Look in the Hotel perhaps the men are in the bar.

EDITOR'S NOTE: To the older residents of Tintern there will be no problem to identify those referred to, or to solving the cryptic puzzles!

TOURISM

By Julian E Ll White

Tourism ranks among the more recent of industries and perhaps the second half of this century has seen an unparalleled development in this field using a variety of techniques and attractions. In many respects Tintern is favourably placed to play a major part in the increasing tourist market.

Two factors, the natural beauty of the area and a pervading sense of history (epitomised in the Abbey), would appear to command attention.

The lower Wye Valley has been designated as an Area of Outstanding Natural Beauty and the reasons become obvious to even the most casual of urban dwellers. The meandering river Wye cloaked with forest covered hills readily conveys an impression of enchantment. Upon arrival the tourist will find his needs well catered for. The serious walker will be keen to explore the Offa's Dyke Walk and the Wye Valley Walk and those of a more perverse nature will relish the challenge which the Devil's Pulpit affords.

In recent years there has been a high standard of service offered by hotels, guest houses, public houses and craft and antique business premises. The tourist will find that a comprehensive package exists to enhance their visit.

The historical aspect in Tintern's tourist appeal is dominated by the famous Abbey. A number of specialist publications are available which provide a thorough interpretation of this monument which is in the care of CADW: Welsh Historic Monuments. Whilst the historical and educational importance of the abbey is soon realised we should also consider that the cultural and artistic dimensions provide fertile grounds for the discerning tourist. It is small wonder that the annual figure for visitors to the abbey stand in excess of 100,000.

The Romantic Movement re-kindled a widespread interest in the abbey, drawing to it many of the most celebrated artists and creative personalities of the age. William Wordsworth, Coleridge and Turner were just three who captured this artistic and poetical ethos. Inspired by these ruins, their craft, and that of others, created a lasting interest in this potent site. It must be said however that for all its charm and beauty Tintern Abbey did not escape artistic criticism. The Reverend

William Gilpin writing in 1782 passed this comment after some consideration: "Tintern Abbey . . . might be made more picturesque by a little judicious demolition. Though parts are beautiful, the whole is ill-shaped . . . a mallet judiciously used (but who durst use it?) might be of service". In some small way his wish was not ignored as many a clandestine mallet was used in order to procure materials to furnish other dwellings in the village.

If the abbey is at the centre of Tintern's historical interest and tourist potential then we should be reminded that there exists also the important aspect of the areas industrial background (in part resulting from the abbey's presence) which will reward the visitor.

The history of the river as a means of transport and communication; the legacy of the wire-works and brass working all contribute to the richness waiting to be re-discovered by a new generation who recognise the value of the commercial history of a community.

One might well argue that the first tourists to the area took the unlikely guise of pilgrims on a spiritual journey which involved stopping at the abbey. Their intention of course was religious and yet even in this we may detect the seeds of provision of facilities which were in demand by those who were non resident and passing through. Hospitality in these circumstances was certainly offered by the abbey foundation and yet it is not preposterous to presume that at this early stage additional or alternative comforts were being offered in the village. This, coupled with the fact that local residents and affiliated workers doubtless looked for refreshment and conviviality suggests that the large number of recorded taverns were established for this purpose.

The present day tourist will have no difficulty in slaking their thirst in the large number of licensed premises in the village. A look in to the past will provide evidence of an even greater number with the implication that tourists, in one form or another, increase the demand for such services. I am indebted to Ivor Waters ("Inns and Taverns of Chepstow and the Lower Wye Valley") for the following information on this point.

ABBEY INN In existence in 1806 no longer in evidence.
ANCHOR INN 1806 to present day.
BEAUFORT ARMS 1781 to present day.
BUTCHER'S ARMS 1857 - 1880.
CARPENTER'S ARMS 1835 - to present day
(now the Wye Valley Hotel).
CHERRY TREE 1852 - to present day.
(Base of Oddfellows, Royal Victoria Lodge 1868)

THE GLOBE 1871 - 1910.
KINGS HEAD 1835 - 1860
MASONS' ARMS 1847 - 1948.
Renamed by the Landlord, Dr Blackford, a psychiatrist, The Moon and Sixpence.
NEW INN 1835 - 1844
NEW GEORGE 1877
(not to be confused with the Royal George)
ROSE AND CROWN 1835 - present
(1841 "Cleanliness of the linen and the promptitude and courtesy of the Landlady"). Also the base of the Oddfellows, Pride of the Wye Lodge, 1863 - 1922 and home to the Tintern Abbey Friendly Society 1904).
ROYAL GEORGE 1835 - present
SHIP INN 1850 - 1900.
Situated in the abbey ruins opposite Saint Annes'.

The predominate drink in the village, up to the turn of the century, was cider, which was homemade. Everywhere, there where cider apple orchards-a few straggly trees remain, as do some of the cider mills.

Charles Harper, a London printer, spent an Autumn holiday touring the Wye Valley during the 1890's, and as a result, he published a book "The Marches of Wales" in 1894. He spent a week in Tintern, and wrote:

". . . mellow Autumn crept on, while the countryside reeked with the sweet smell of pomace, and cider making went forward in all the fruitful orchards round about. Before almost every cottage door were barrels and hogsheads, kilderkins and puncheons, filled or being filled with fresh cider".

The locality of Tintern may have presented problems to the tourist until recent times. For many years the easiest mode of travel was probably by river to the region. There is evidence that this fact was incorporated into the entrepreneurial thinking of the day. Our cultural vandal, Reverend Gilpin, and others, can be counted among the forerunners of Tourist Traders in that they organised river trips to Tintern with the passage endued with requisite food and music. It was perhaps unfortunate that these well planned excursions, a genteel drift down the Wye, to the accompaniment of the harp, was oftern rudely shattered by the oaths and colourful language of the river-bank dwellers. Gilpin, who was troubled by this behaviour may have been pleased to learn (looking down we presume from some heavenly abode) that the situation had been reversed by the 1890's. About this time we learn that day trippers from Birmingham and the Black Country were causing no end of upset and trouble to the locals, but then, these visitors arrived by rail which may account for the situation!

Coxe and the poet Thomas Gray were among the more distinguished company who travelled on the Wye for pleasure. The journey appears to have been made either from Ross to Chepstow, or from Bristol, and thence upstream to Piercefield and Tintern.

The improvement of roads and the increased use of motor transport made Tintern more accessible and popular. Charabanc tours in the vicinity are still recalled with pleasure, and one of the prime motives of the visitor was to experience the view of the harvest moon rising throught the rose window of the abbey. The Gloucester Journal, of September 1883, confirms that this custom was much in practice even before mechanised transport was widely available: "on the night of the Harvest Moon, 500 to 600 people from Gloucester and Cheltenham visited by excursion train". Similar trips started out from the Newport and Cardiff areas and it was no uncommon thing for Tintern to act as host for 1300 people or more. On these figures one can begin to appreciate the reason for so many taverns in the small community.

The coming of the railway in 1876 further opened the way for the growth of tourism in Tintern. A visit to the abbey was becoming less of a privileged undertaking as in Gilpin's day and more of a family outing within the budget of most people. The rail trip from Chepstow to Monmouth has been described as "one of the most beautiful journeys in Britain". With the benefit of hind-sight it appears now that the closing of the line in 1959 was an ill considered decision which not only resulted in considerable inconveniece to the local population but a retrograde step in the interests of tourism, blossoming as it has done, in the few years since the line was discontinued. It is ironical that Tintern Station is now a tourist attraction in its own right rather than taking an active part in the transportation of visitors to and from the many other sites of interest and tourist potential.

Historians will note that freight continued to be carried through Tintern by rail until 1964. In its heyday Tintern Station serviced four or five trains a day with summer excursions to London, Birmingham and Cardiff. From Chepstow to Monmouth the journey lasted approximately 50 minutes with twelve stops and the cost of a return was 2/9 (14p) in 1957. Tintern also had a goods yard, engine shed and sidings.

The scope and potential of tourism in general is now widely acknowledged. The search continues to find yet another different slant to marketing an area or site and Tintern is little different from other venues in this respect.

Above all else, save perhaps for the beauty of the area, it is the historical dimension of Tintern that provides the initial attraction. It is not surprising therefore to find a visitor asking whether Tintern can lay claim to its own ghost, haunting, or other such supernatural event.

Again it is the Abbey which arouses curiousity in this respect. On a bright summer morning, sharing the ruin with hundreds of other visitors and their chatter, it is difficult to imagine anything more sinister than an empty crisp packet scudding through the cloisters. On a cold, grey and lonely winters evening it is different.

Some years ago, the story goes, an unknown woman was in the habit of taking up a position in the outer parlour. She was unknown, except that the powers of a medium were accredited to her, and her hours passed in waiting for the spirits of the dead to make contact with her. As dusk fell on the evening of the harvest moon, a coldness coursed through her body and a profound silence fell upon the hunched ruins. She became aware at length that a shadow, darker than those which gathered about the walls, stood before her. Stood indeed, for the shape was that of a man. The figure had about it an air of infinite weariness and sorrow, tempered only by a restlessness which flickered and burned in the empty sockets of its skeletal face. The apparition grew less indistinct and the woman saw that she was confronted by an emaciated figure in stained and bloody armour. Although the dry lips appeared not to move, a rasping whisper reached her and filled her head with icy echoes:

"the task is done, the duty carried through; give me my rest, by all that is sacred, bury me". The darkness rushed in upon the woman and the blackness heaved with the sound and half formed images of battle, violence and the stench of death. Abruptly the quietness returned; it was a cold evening with the Harvest Moon pouring it's light through the rose window of the Abbey. And where the light fell, where there had been nothing before, a rose now lay on the ground, blood red.

The tale now becomes vague, but local opinion has it that the ghost was that of a knight slain in some bloody conflict at an unspecified date close to the abbey. The circumstances were such that the body was buried in haste and secrecy in an open field, and there it should have ended. The spirits of the dead are frequently restless however, and this one cried down the ages his one request - to be buried in consecrated ground.

Local legend has it that the woman was led to the remains of the knight which she brought out from its desolate confines, and re-interred at some location within the consecrated abbey building.

The truth of this cannot be vouched for. It is only known that on certain occasions, a blood red rose is to be found laid tenderly on the spot where the light from the Harvest Moon falls.

A story without foundation? Perhaps; but it was in far more recent times that a stone coffin denoting a burial of someone of rank was inadvertantly uncovered in a nearby field. It was empty.

Another long standing tradition will have it that the ghost of a "White Monk" can be seen traversing in the Abbey ruins.

Across from the Abbey lies the ruined church of Saint Mary. In recent years some villagers have sworn to seeing an unearthly light illuminating what remains of the building and the surrounding area.

Other accounts tell of a certain gate near the Fountain Inn which many people fear to walk past. In a similar fashion there is said to be an unwholesome atmosphere to be found in an upstairs room of Orchard Cottage.

Reputed hauntings in Tintern are not confined to human spirits. Local talk maintains that should you be walking up the Angidy Valley at night, you may well encounter a black dog sitting in the road, where it forks not far from the Cherry Tree. As the walker approaches the dog disappears; timid souls will retrace their steps while those of sterner stuff will press on - with speed - to the sanctuary of the Cherry Tree.

There is no reason to suppose that Tintern will not increase its tourist potential. The natural beauty, history, facilities, friendliness and ease of access surely point to a busy and varied future for the area.

◆ ◆ ◆ ◆

Because, for centuries, Tintern has sat on the border of England and Wales, and because the Welsh language has not been spoken in the valley for over one hundred years, it is easy to overlook the fact that the origins of this village are Welsh. So it is particularly interesting to have come across the following article, printed in our Parish Magazine a few years ago.

NEW YEAR GIFT

Reading an article in a local paper recently brought back memories of when I came to Tintern some forty odd years ago.

On 1 January we used to receive a "New Year Gift". This, as I recall, consisted of a medium size apple (any sort) with pieces of green box hedging pushed into the top with a few hazel nuts attached. Three wooden skewers, to form legs, were pushed into the bottom of the apple so that it could be stood up on the mantlepiece. It was decreed that it should remain there until the apple rotted, thus making sure of a happy New Year. I remember Vivien and Bernard Lawrence bringing these gifts and have checked my recollection with their mother, Mrs Dorothy Lawrence, who tells me that they used to make about 20 - all who received them were thrilled to have them. The boy had to have dark hair and be let in by the front door and leave by the back.

In Tintern the gift was known simply as a "New Year Gift" but I understand it was the old Welsh custom of making a "Monty" or Calennig.

TINTERN - ROUND AND ABOUT

By Judith Russill

Until the turn of this century, Tintern comprised two parishes - Chapel Hill to the south, and Tintern Parva at the northern end. The combined parishes are full of interest, and to hopefully avoid confusion, I intend to divide the area into sections, so as best to describe all that there is to see.

APPROACHING THE VILLAGE As you enter the parish of Tintern, travelling from Chepstow along the A466, you pass the Livox Farm on your right, the name being a corruption of "Live Oaks". The road becomes wooded, and is reputedly haunted by the ghost of a young maiden, who, having been ravished, was pushed into a fissure in the rocks. Her skeleton was found towards the end of the eighteenth century when men were blasting for lime-stone. Way down, on the side of the River Wye, are the remains of an ancient *piscatory*, once belonging to the Abbey, and local knowledge has it that here the monks had a pond in which to keep their salmon. Close by is the *cold well*, a stone drain into which flows the surface water of a green lane and the ooze from two springs.

Opposite the Livox Quarry, in the woods, are two *lime kilns*. In these, lime stone was burnt, having first been mixed with wood. The resulting quick lime was used in the making of mortar and as a valuable fertiliser. It was also used in the process of tanning.

Further along the main road, on the left, is the *linen well*. About twenty years ago, the main road was widened, and the well moved back some six feet. The origin of its name is unknown, maybe clothes were washed here, but it was used to water the horses travelling along the road. Some forty years ago, in a cave behind the well, there lived a tramp, known locally as "Bill Buggs Hole". Bill would travel the countryside with his belongings in an old sack, and was often to be seen entertaining the tourists, outside the Anchor. He would play the tin whistle, sometimes with his nose, and the few pennies that Bill earned would buy him a pint of beer!

Next, you pass Reddings Farm, the name once being that of one of the Abbeys' granges. Just before reaching the Beaufort Hotel, way up on your left, stood Cliff Cottage, now demolished. The woods above, are known as *lime kiln woods*, two more kilns being here. Once, they were called *colwell grove*, after the Cold Well situated on the side of the old Coach Road. This runs up the valley, behind the Beaufort Hotel, and was the way into the village, before the main road was built last century.

ABBY TINTERN - the flattish area that you now reach, below St Mary's Church, as far as the Angidy River, (which once formed the boundary between Chapel Hill and Tintern Parva,) and then down to the rivers edge was once known as Abby Tintern. An inn, called the *Beaufort,* has existed here for centuries. During the eighteenth century, the Gethin family lived here. The family was widespread in the lower Wye Valley, and much involved in the river trade. George Gethin, senior, combined the occupations of victualler with those of mariner and shipowner. But by the end of the century, his sons, Robert and George, had moved to Newport where they founded a prosperous coasting line. So, when George senior died, the Inn was taken over by Mr Mitchel, who also held the keys to the Abbey. By 1811, the Inn was described as "neat and comfortable", and Mrs Mitchel was happy to provide the where-withal for a picnic in the Abbey. After the first World War the, by now, Beaufort Hotel was run by a colourful figure, Captain Sharp. An active member of the British Legion, he instigated an Annual Parade. He ran the best dance band in the locality, known as the *hush* Band. Another of his interests was the Otter Hounds, of which he was Master. Hunting near Bigsweir Bridge, he found an otter cub, which he brought home. A pond was dug for Bella, and by it was placed a collecting box for the Legion's funds. Captain Sharp was often to be seen walking with Bella on a lead, and as she would return to his call, he would unleash her so that she could swim in the Angidy. The publican at The Anchor , Mr Radelli, not to be outdone, asked Arthur Mackie to catch a fox that lived near his home. This poor creature was kept chained on the lawn. In time, Bella escaped, and not long after the fox, too, had gone, no doubt set free by some kind soul. However, on his way home, the fox broke into Wilf Jones, the butcher at the Gwyn Stores, and killed all the chickens.

Next door to the hotel is an imposing house called *St Anne's House*. Directly opposite the Abbey was the Gatehouse, leading onto the old coach road, and St Anne's was the Chapel of the Gatehouse. The house, as seen today, was largely rebuilt during the last century, but incorporates in it parts of the old Chapel. On the eastern side of the house, three lancet windows are plainly visible. The Chapel is known to have been in existence during the fourteenth century, and on the north-east side can be seen a fragment of old wall and the springing of a vaulted roof. A famous occupant of St Anne's was John Loraine Baldwin, who died in 1896, aged 92. He was a founder member of the famous I Zingari Cricket Club, and a well-known Society figure of his day. From 1873, until his death, he was Warden of the Abbey. His funeral, taking place on a wet Tuesday afternoon, was a grand affair, attended by several members of the Aristocracy. The cortege left for St Michael's Church, (where his wife, Elizabeth, Lady Francis Russell had been buried in 1888,) lead by the local police. The hearse was followed by "the deceased's valet who had during a lengthy servitude become greatly attached to his master". Then followed eight coaches, including one for the servants. Eight members of the clergy officiated at the service, including the Rector of Tintern Parva, The Reverend H B Hennell. According to the Chepstow Weekly Advertiser, which reported the funeral, "The Church had been prettily decorated with white chrysanthemums, and evergreens . . . . the surpliced choir was assisted by Mr E Palmer on the cornet and Miss Finch on the organ . . . . the brick-lined vault had been tastily lined with Chrysanthemums, moss and evergreens". There were sixty eight wreaths, including one from George, H.R.H. Duke of Cambridge, and one from the "Cottagers and Inhabitants of Tintern and Chapel Hill! St Anne's was once surrounded by ancient walnut trees, but by 1841, only one remained.

The area beyond St Anne's House was once an orchard. The

pair of stone houses, known as Upper Leytons, were built at the turn of this century, and Abbey Antiques is built on the site of one of several blacksmith's shops once found in the village. As early as 1564, this site was known as *the leytons*, and still, today, the sports field, below, is called by this name. Running behind is Chapel Lane, and just above Upper Leytons, on the opposite side of the lane, is a walled enclosure, once the *village pound* where stray animals were placed until claimed by their owners. The ruins of *St Mary's Church* are reached by a steep stone path. The churchyard is still used for funerals, and on such occasions reached with difficulty. Earlier this century, it was the custom, at a funeral, for the mourners to gather at the deceased's house, where a short service of hymns and prayers was held. Teams of bearers would then carry the coffin to the church, changing every few hundred yards or so. Along the route (always the road, never the tracks), blinds would have been drawn in the houses as a mark of respect. During the service, the bell would be tolled once a minute, to remind the village that one of their number was no longer with them. On a happier occasion, at weddings, local lads would tie the church gates together, and the happy couple would have to pay a toll of about 6d to be let out! The stone stocks once stood in this churchyard, but have now disappeared.

The junction of three roads with the main road is known as Tintern Cross, and there were a couple of cottages situated opposite Abbey Antiques, roughly where the concrete slab stands. Here, too, was a large may tree, under which couples courted! On the small green once stood a horse trough.

Cross the road to the *Royal George Hotel.* The early part of the hotel was built in 1598. A stone slab, over a side door, once bore the marks TB and the date, but these have now weathered away. Fortunately, a sketch remains to show that it existed! When Richard White took over the Wire Works, in 1704, he decided to live in the village, and enlarged the house standing on this site, and here he entertained the more notable visitors to the Abbey. The car park of the hotel is partly built on the site of a pond, very evident after heavy rain, when the pond tries to establish its original boundaries. The pond is clearly shown in early postcards.

Having reached the Angidy River, cross the road to *Abbey Mill.* A mill has stood here for centuries, and was certainly used by the Abbey. At sometime during the sixteenth and seventeenth centuries, one of the several Wire Mills in the Angidy Valley was started here. Not so very long ago, the river was providing the power for lathes and saws, as during this century, the mill was used as a Saw Mill and builder's yard, by one of the several Jones families in the village. The dock can still be seen, and John Jones cleaned it out so as to bring timber in by barge. The builders yard closed in the seventies, and the site has recently been developed as a Craft Shop complex.

Now start walking back towards the Abbey. *Abbey House*, now an art gallery, and until recently, the Police Station, stands on the site of an earlier building of the same name, demolished at the start of the century. The earlier Abbey House was the home of Iron Masters, during the last century, including Jeremiah Sharp Browne and Henry Hughes. When rebuilt, the middle section opened as Abbey Stores, one of several Grocers in the village, which closed not so very long ago.

Bear left, in front of the Police Station, passing the Community Hall built to commemorate the Queen's Jubilee. A pair of stone houses, Lower Leytons, match those on Chapel Lane. Straight in front is a row of bungalows for the elderly, built on the site of a saw mill and breeze-block factory, run by the Floyd family. It is possible that this was previously the site of the Abbey's tannery, as it is stated that this was on the edge of the river.

The Methodist Church was built in 1861, on the site of a cottage, workshop and coal yard belonging to a shoemaker, William Lee. The site was bought for £60, the main instigator being the local maltster, George Roberts. One of the masons employed was a Mr Moulton, and his grandson, Mr W J Pickering who now lives in one of the adjoining bungalows! According to the Religious Census of 1851, there was a Wesleyan Methodist Church, erected in 1820, but the site of this is unknown. The social life of the Methodist Church is well remembered by Mr Ray Waite who, as a lad enjoyed the annual outing to Porthcawl or Barry. Sometimes they took the train to Tidenham, and then walked to Beachley, and on other occasions, the children just crossed the bridge to Ferry Farm, where they had tea and played games in the field. The Christmas Tea was also a highspot.

Quay Cottages have stood witness for several hundred years, as has *Quay House.* In front of Quay Cottages, a slip once ran down into the river, and can be seen in photographs taken earlier this century.

Quay House was once the home of the Quay Master, when the riverside between the Angidy and the Abbey was a bustling wharf. It is difficult to assess the age of the house, maybe as old as the

1760's, though a National Monuments record infers that parts could date from the 1400's. During the last century, it became a carpenter's workshop. In more recent years, villagers remember it as a sweet shop, where the children spent half their Collection, before going to Church on a Sunday morning, until found out! During the 1970's, whilst an extension was being built, a lime-pit still containing slaked lime was uncovered. This could well have been part of the nearby tannery, as the lime pits were used during the process of cleaning the hides. Another important ingredient of tanning was Oak Bark, and just along the path from Quay House, you come to a long stone building, now a guest house, but once the *Bark Yard*. This too, is an ancient building, maybe as much as four hundred years old. In the 1880's, the bark cutters were still at work here, chopping the bark before loading it onto the trows which would have moored along side. A more notorious use was as a temporary morgue for those poor unfortunates found drowned in the river. Here, too, the Hopkins family ran their prosperous Cooper's Yard.

Continue along the old cartroad, once the only way the drays could reach the Anchor. On the right, between the track and the playing fields, a rough area used to be tennis courts! *The Anchor* has, for centuries, provided sustenance for the traveller, especially those waiting for the *Ferry*, to cross to the other side of the Wye. The ancient Water Gate of the Abbey can still be seen, though sadly, the old slipway has been filled in. However, if you stand on the edge, you can just see the end, at low tide. The ferry ceased to operate after the First World War, and there had been a Ferryman in the village since the fourteenth century, if not before. Directly opposite the Water Gate, on the Gloucester bank, you can see the remains of a stone quay at low tide. From here ran a cobbled track, no longer in existence, towards the site of the now demolished Ferry Farm. From there, one made one's way up the Abbey Passage and across to Brockweir, where the monks had a farm.

The area between the Anchor and the Abbey is now open, but once was covered in small cottages, many remembered by older villagers. This part was known as *Wyeside*, with as many as twelve cottages from here to Abbey Farm, including four Poor Houses. One of the Wyeside cottages was *Ship Cottage,* where Mr and Mrs Ted Wheeler started their married life. Ted's grandfather and great-grandfather, both salmon fishermen, had lived there, roughly on the site of the Abbot's Hall. His grandfather, John, later ran the *Ship Inn* which was built on the site of the Abbey Guest House. John had taken over the Inn from his father-in-law, William Tamplin, in the

1870's. During the 1920s-1930s, visitors would flock to Tintern on the night of the Harvest Moon, to witness the moon rising behind the Great Window of the Abbey. Many were none too welcome, as they would take more than memories home with them! They came equipped with pillowcases into which they stowed their ill-gotten gains. The orchards were raided, and the locals made sure that their doors were locked that night. Close to the Ship Inn was Abbey Gate Cottage, which became a Refreshment and Coffee Room during the 1860s. This area of cottages, roughly where the carparks are, was known as Old Abbey. If I neglect the *Abbey* in this book, no slur is intended, but one can pick up any number of books and read about its history. To add more would be superfluous. Suffice it to say that its coming, existence and dissolution has had an enormous impact upon this community, and still has today, as a tourist attraction. In the late seventeenth century, Gilpin, and others, make much of the peasants living in squalor amongst the ruins. It would seem that as late as the 1880s, people were still living in makeshift structures. Mr Sid Jones recalls that his stepmother spoke of having seen no less that thirteen people "existing" there. Before the last War, Mr Waite remembers that three to four men were employed at the Abbey, just to keep the stone work in order. There is an old mine, painted red, in the car park. Under here, there used to be steps leading to a passage. Mr Wheeler remembers going down here, and is of the opinion that once a passage linked the Abbey with the Manor House.

Return now to the main road, and walk back to the Cross.

THE ANGIDY VALLEY As you turn into this valley, to the left of The George, the first cottage you see, up on your left, is *Walnut Tree Cottage.* Sid Jones remembers when Dr Bartlett lived here, and his Dispensary was built onto the side. Apparently all the bottles were filled with three different coloured liquids but all Epsom Salts! Dr Bartlett brought a number of older villagers into this world, and is remembered for his shiny leggings, stick and bowler hat! Just beyond, where Crown Lodge stands, was another Blacksmiths.

The next building, recently converted to a dwelling, was the *Village School.* The inhabitants of Tintern have had the advantage of education for over three hundred years. In the latter half of the seventeenth century, the Wire Works Company had, on its payroll, a preacher earning £8 per annum, and a Master, in charge of the Works School, earning 40/- per annum. On 2 May, 1704, the Bishop admitted Thomas Richards to exercise the Office of Schoolmaster in Chapel Hill. The National School was established around 1818, in a room rented from the Duke of Beaufort. After much delay, a new School was built in 1839, and in the Lascelles Directory for 1852, we read that the school was supported by Subscription and the children's pence. The Master was Mr David Cornfield, assisted by his wife. By 1862, their daughter, Mary Ann, had taken over. She was also the organist for St Mary's Church - this joint task was continued by many successive schoolmasters. One of the Friendly Societies had its headquarters at the school room - The National Deposit Society, and the agent was Mr William Jones. By the nineteen hundreds, the Schoolmaster was Mr T C Alexander, still remembered. The first radio in the village was a Crystal Set, made by his son. Mr Alexander was Vicars' Warden and a lay reader, and often organised plays and concerts in the parish rooms. The School Inspector, Totty Jenkins, came from Chepstow to check that all the children were in school, and woe betide them if they were found playing truant! The Vicar, Mr Washington-Palmer always talked to the children on Fridays - frequently his topic was "The Dangers of Alcohol". The children were given days off for gathering whinberries, and during the First World War, they also had days off to gather horse chestnuts which apparently were an ingredient in explosives! The whole school attended Church on Ascension Day, and then had the rest of the day off. Lunch hour lasted for an hour and twenty minutes. Mr Waite recalls that lunch was eaten hastily, and then all the children went off to play. Games seemed to be played according to season, Tip Cat, Marbles, Rounders and Fox and Hounds. Then the bell sounded, and back to school for the afternoon. Sometimes, in the winter, school was closed for several weeks because of the outbreaks of infection. In 1913, Class I walked to Chepstow and back, to see an exhibition and to hear a lecture on Tuberculosis. Another walk to Chepstow happened on 25 May, 1920, to witness the launching of the "War Glory", the first of the "N" types to be launched by the Monmouth Shipping Company. The Angidy Valley is occasionally ravaged by storms, and on the 22 September, 1935, a particularly severe one caused the river to burst its' banks. A small stream also runs behind the school, and this brought down hundreds of tons of stone and mud, wrecking the playground. There were similar problems in 1981. Four years before the school closed, the children took part in a tableau, dressed as monks, to celebrate the 850th Anniversary of the Founding of Tintern Abbey. The date: Saturday 9 May, 1981 - the precise anniversary.

It all came to an end in 1985, when with great sadness the School finally closed.

Just beyond the School, you come to Pitch House, bearing a plaque dated 1699, and the initials EF. These were, I suspect, the initials of Edward Fisher, the Fishers having lived in the valley for centuries. This house is supposed to have been the house for the Manager of the Mill opposite. In the Census Returns of 1841-1881, it is always referred to as "Old House Grounds". Opposite is the *Mill House,* predominantly Victorian, but with seventeenth century origins. The road forks just below the *Cherry Tree Inn*. Taking the right fork, up on the left is *Gwyn House*. This, in the seventeenth century, was the residence of John Gwyn, and invariably was occupied by the manager of the Wire Works. John Gwyn's ancestor arrived in Tintern during the sixteenth century, acting as Steward for the Duchess of Worcester. The date of the original building is unclear, but a downstairs room with oak beams looks to be very old, and certainly predates the rest of the property, which was built by Thomas Gwyn and his wife, Debrah Young. Later, the Gwyns moved to Porthcasseg, where they continued to act as Stewards for the Beaufort family. The house changed hands many times, and in 1836, the owner was John Rowbotham, shipper and manager of the Works. In 1903, it was put up for auction and sold for £320! Part of the house is now the Cherry Tree Inn.

A little further up the hill, in Forge Road, was *The Bible Christians' Chapel* known as *The Ark*. The Religious Census of 1851 states that the Bible Christians had been meeting in a private house since before 1800, and had been unable to find land on which to build a church. Once a branch of the Baptist Church, it later became allied to the Methodist. It finally closed in 1922, and was sold in 1942 for £150. It is now Chapel Garage. The Bible Christians also had their own Friendly Society, the Ark Society, meeting in the vestry with Mrs Pritchard as secretary.

Just above is *Valley House,* old but of uncertain age. It proudly boasts a twin-seater privy. Now run as a guest house, I believe that more up to date sanitation is offered ! The Angidy runs under this house, and when the river is in flood, you can hear boulders crashing around.

A number of small roads lead off Forge Road, leading up to the Cot, The Bantams and Fair Oak Farm. These roads were still unmade in the early part of this century. The heavy timber wagons came down from the hills. With the wooden brakes applied, they slid down, leaving nine inch deep ruts. When these filled with rain, the children sailed their toy boats in them. Occasionally, the roads were rolled smooth by a steam roller. Mr Waite remembers going, as a small boy, up to the Bantams with his aunts. This was at Christmas, at midnight, when it was believed one would see the rosemary bloom and the cows kneel.

Right at the top of the Angidy Valley, you come to a "T" junction, known as *Pont-y-Saeson*. This was also known as Tintern Cross. Whether there was a Cross here, or whether the name derives from a cross road is a matter for speculation. However, at this point, parallel to the lane leading to the Fountain Inn, is an old lane of great antiquity. Here, at Pont-y-Saeson, is the site of the Upper Forge, and nearby, the Howell family ran a small pub, probably little more than a cider house. The men folk were also plasterers and masons, advertising their skills in the various Directories of the last Century. It was a Charles Howell, of this family, who was foreman of the great landscaping works of Piercefield House.

To the left of Pont-y-Saeson, up in the woods is an area known as Gethin's Grove. At the time of the Dissolution of the Abbey, one of the monks was a John Gethin. He later was in dispute with the former abbot, Wyche, over an annuity from the proceeds of an area of land near Trellech Grange. Maybe, this piece of the wood is the disputed land, hence the name.

Returning back down the valley, passing the Old Furnace, there are several cottages close to the river. The 1841 census mentions a Victoria Inn close to here, but there is no precise knowledge as to its location.

Near to Valley House, you may have missed an old house set way back off the road, as you walked up previously. This was the *Globe*, yet another of Tintern's Inns! It is now a private house, having closed in 1906, but was more of a cider house than an Inn. Attached to the side, was a small grocer's shop. The Globe was run by Mr Frank Wheeler, father of Ted. A great character who was always to be seen doing something in the village. He had a pony and trap in which he would deliver oil and candles. He gardened, built stone walls, "layed" hedges, and was also the Insurance Agent. He was devoted to St Mary's Church, and in the 1950s, stood outside the Abbey and collected £200 to pay for the re-roofing of the church. He is also remembered as the grave digger. On Palm Sunday, the Welsh custom of decorating the graves with flowers is still observed. Known here as Flower Sunday, overnight the church-yards blossom into colour. When Mr Ted Wheeler left school, he joined the GWR, and, for a spell, worked at Tintern Station. Whilst living in the village he was secretary of the Nursing Association. A 1d was collected each week from participants, and this paid for a resident Nurse/Midwife in the village during the 1930s. Ted remembers a Sunday School Outing, in 1911, when three large boats, hired from Chepstow, each carried thirty people to Beachley. Skippered by Frank Wheeler, Mr Pickering and Percy Coy, they left at 9.00 am. Ted recalls how lovely it was on the Wye, but rather choppy on the Severn! They returned in darkness, on the tide.

Mr Ray Waite remembers an old man, Mr Writtle, who worked in the Saw Mill opposite Pitch House. He used to make hoops from split hazel, for dry casks, spiggots and tent pegs. A sack of shavings could be bought for 1d as kindling.

By now, you will have once more reached the George, so turn left, and enter the old parish of Tintern Parva.

THROUGH THE VILLAGE Crossing the Angidy River, an old cottage can be seen on the left, known as The Bay. Way above, is The Rock, and beyond, following the paths back up the Angidy Valley, there was once a pub called the Carpenters Arms. Once, there were three of that name in Tintern! Opposite the Bay is the Surgery, where once was yet another Blacksmiths. Behind is a large brick and corrugated iron building, which was, until fairly recently, the Parish Rooms. This for many years provided a spendid venue for village events, particularly excellent Nativity Plays, and each winter, a Pageant when, Mr Wheeler tells me, all the countries of the Commonwealth were represented by villagers wearing authentic costumes.

The Parish Rooms lie along side the Wye, and it is possibly here that the *Ford* was sited. There was certainly a ford in Roman times, as they used it to cross the Wye before they constructed the wooden bridge at Chepstow. As there was a Roman camp just below Madgett's Farm, in Brockweir, it has been suggested that the ford was here, just half a mile above the village. However, there is no evidence of ancient tracks leading to and from the river at this point. At low water, during the drier months of the summer, it is possible to ford the river just above the old tramway bridge, in Tintern village itself. This is a much more likely site for the Romans to use, marching across from Gloucester, over the river and then up the Angidy valley to join the known Roman track, and then onwards to Usk.

Back on the left hand side of the road, the tea shop was once a grocers, and next door, the building now housing Monks' Optics was Ashweir House, and classified in the last century as a home of the gentry! Past the old and long established pub, the *Rose and Crown*, you arrive at Melrose Cottage, at various times in the last century a Temperance Hotel and a Ladies Seminary. Wesley Cottage belonged to the Methodist Church, hence its name. It had been owned by the Roberts family, and was willed to the Church by William Roberts, tailor, brother of the maltsters John and George, in 1867. It was sold prior to the 1920s.

Further along, next to the newsagents, is an old cottage. As Stow Cottage, it was the village lock-up. It then became the Police Station in the 1850s. Thomas Griffiths was Police Constable in 1861, and by 1871, the village was safely in the hands of P.C. Mugglesworth.

The long building, now housing the antique shop, Belle View House and the Post Office, was once a Malthouse, home of John and George Roberts. It later became a Grocers and Bakery.

The *Falls Guest House* for many years was called *Strathwye.* Here lived the village doctor for some forty years, during the last century, John Audland at first, and then Doctors Brown and Kay. The cottage opposite was the coach house. Miss Marjorie Thomas well remembers being there on the 22 September, 1935. At midnight, a tremendous storm broke, and the South Wales Argus of the Monday following, reports that hailstones, the size of walnuts, blocked the road to Chepstow, taking all day to clear. The storm was so great, it forced the waterfall, behind the house, to change course, and the house was flooded. The Beaufort Hotel was also badly affected, and only Captain Sharp's quick thinking prevented worse damage. As it was, the stewards' room was flooded with five feet of water. But, back to Strathwye, the early part of the house was built in 1755, and at the end of the garden can be seen the remains of the stables and a smithy. It has been a guest house since the 1920s.

Next we come to a modern house built on the site of Wye Cottage, once the home of a fisherman called Edward Tamplin.

Prospect Cottage was the home of Hannah Luff in 1871. She and her daughter Margaret, ran a lodging house, and in 1881 was known as the Temperance Hotel. It too, was the Post Office! Next door, from as early as 1841, lived one of the many Waite families. By the 1880s, Matilda Waite had turned the garden of Spring Cottage into a tea garden.

The Moon and Sixpence, was until after the last war known as *The Masons Arms*. During the 1930's, it was run by Mr Watkins, owner of the first car in the village, which he used to collect people from the railway station. Opposite, is the Tintern Garage, and David

Hunt's Butcher's Shop. This had been built as a Malthouse, and the car park adjacent is remembered as a wharf by older residents. If you stand on the edge of the river, and look along the building, you will see several projecting iron girders, used for the loading of boats. During the 1930s, many a happy evening was spent upstairs, as here was sited the Cinema. Run by Mr Watkins, from over the road, it cost 3d. Later, on a Saturday evening, between seven and ten, a whist drive was held, and after that, from ten thirty until two in the morning, a dance - costing 1/6.

The *Old Rectory* was previously called *Springwell.* A very old cottage has been extended to the house you see today. It would seem that the Rector lived here from the middle of the 1800s, when the Reverend John Mais was the incumbent. Mr Ted Wheeler has many memories of the Reverend A W Washington Palmer. A great character who had planned on being a musician until becoming deaf. Instead, he took Holy Orders. An excellent organist, his recitals were most popular, the villagers' favourite being "The Nightingale and the Canary". As an elderly man, he found it difficult to climb up to St Mary's, so he paid Frank Wheeler and Henry Jones, the coalman, 2/6 each to carry him up in a bamboo chair! Behind the house is a series of lawns, a popular venue for croquet and garden parties. In the winter, the Church Choir was entertained to the Annual Supper - the high spot being the fifty Gold Flake cigarettes supplied for the occasion! In those days, the organist was Mr Hartley. Christmas Day was a "big" day for the choir - the master gave each boy 3d and the Rector gave 6d!

On the other side of the road, beyond the garage was another blacksmith, and for many years, in the last century, William Page plied his trade here.

Next door to the Old Rectory is the *Manor House*. Though the present house is Victorian, a house was known to have been here in the early part of the fourteenth century. It is thought that it was built by Elizabeth de Burgh, and it was here that Queen Isabella stayed, when she visited Tintern in 1326. Later, in Tudor times, it was rebuilt and it has been suggested that this was undertaken by the former Abbot of Tintern, Richard Wyche. A drawing of the house, taken from a painting by M E Bagnall-Oakley, appears in Bradneys' "History of Monmouthshire" of 1913. In the middle Ages, the Manor and all its' lands belonged to the Clares, Earls of Gloucester. By the Seventeenth century, Richard Herbert sold it to a kinsman, Thomas. The indenture mentions "one water corn mill with appurtances in Tintern Magna and Tintern Parva, now in the possession of Thomas

Berrington, gentleman, and his wife Tacy", a messuage in the occupation of Robert Smith and another of Elizabeth Jayne. Also, a 200 acre wood called Kebedicke, (Coed Beddig) occupied by John Catchmay, and 6 acres of meadow and 8 acres of pasture in the occupation of Hester and Alice Geathen (Gethin?), plus a parcel of land occupied by George Harris.

During the Civil War, it is believed that Lewis Morris (brother of the founders of Piercefield House), lived here. He was an officer in the Parliamentarian Forces and was present at the siege of Chepstow Castle. On the Restoration of Charles II, in 1660, he went to the West Indies, and then on to America, to New Jersey, where he founded an iron works at Tintern Falls in Monmouth County. Later occupants were William Fielding and his wife, Elizabeth, who is buried in the aisle of St Michael's Church. It is thought that Henry Fielding, the novelist, was a relation and stayed at the Manor House when he wrote "Tom Jones", but there is nothing to support this story. By 1787, the estate was owned by Nathaniel and John Osborne, related by marriage to Richard White of the Wire Works. Edward Davies, a timber merchant, bequeathed the Manor to two brothers by the name of Gale in 1838. For many years, John Gale farmed the Livox. In 1856, they sold off the estate, including the Nurtons and the advowson of the Living, and by 1889, the estate had been broken up. The old, ruined house was demolished, and the existing, smaller property built in its place by Arthur Pontifax Price.

Adjacent to the Manor House is another fine old stone house called the *Hospice*, its name suggesting a connection with the Abbey. Inside, there is a large sixteenth-seventeenth century fireplace with an ashlar surround. On its' iron chimney flue is the date 1618, and the initials PC. John Fryer, a prosperous timber merchant, ship-owner and mariner, came to the Hospice sometime in the 1860s. He operated from the Wharf, by the side of St Michael's Church. Early postcards show a slipway, now filled in. Millstones, made at Whitebrook , where unloaded here. The mill-stones were rolled down Whitebrook valley, and loaded onto trows at Bigsweir. On a day when the water is clear, it is sometimes possible to see stones lying in the bottom of the river, where they failed to make the boat!

Opposite the Hospice was a row of workers cottages, now converted into one house. Known as *Fryers Terrace*, John Fryer built them for his employees. St Michael's Church is picturesquely situated by the side of the river, but, at high tides, it is a little close for comfort. Behind the church is the *Parva Farmhouse*, now a guest house but once the farmhouse of the main farm in Tintern Parva. The main building has recently had an extra storey added to it, but the end closest to the church is the oldest part, having fifteenth century origins. It used to have two gable windows, and was used as the farm dairy, with a granary above.

Cross the road, and look up to the Parva Vineyard, thought to be on the site of the vineyard belonging to the Abbey.

The Wye Valley Hotel used to be called *The Carpenters Arms.* Next door but one is Gothic Cottage. This had once been known as *Hope Cottage*, and in 1889 Miss Louisa Brown ran a tea room here. Look back across the main road, and just to the right of Fryers Row a stone wall surrounds the well where, until the early 1950's, when mains water came to the village, local residents collected their water. In the top of the wall you can see cemented the stone base of an ancient Cross, once sited at this junction. All that is left is a cross-socketed stone with broached corners and a partly destroyed chamfered octagonal upper surface.

ABOVE THE VILLAGE - a high ridge runs alongside the river. Heavily wooded, it hides many cottages. Known as Barbadoes Hill, its name has always been questioned. Some say that it was named after Lewis Morris fled the country and went to that island. But, there is also a "Botany Bay" and a "Maryland" in the village, and another explanation is that, in the late seventeen hundreds, extra labour was needed for the Wire Works, and convicts, who had served and survived their sentence of transportation, were encouraged to settle here, and gave their new homes these names.

Up on this ridge, on the eastern side of Cook's Patch, are a collection of large boulders, marked on the maps as Cairns. Various suggestions have been put forward as to their origin, including Burial Mounds and the site of a beacon. However, topographically, the site is unsuitable for a beacon, being below the summit of the hill. In 1958, a former forester, Mr A E Allen, was interviewed, and he explained that the local name for these were the *Devil's Lap Stones*, and that local tradition indicated that they are the burial mounds of warriors who were killed in battle. They are no great distance from Pont-y-Saeson, site of the great battle against the Saxons. Beyond the Cairns, is a large area of woodland, known as Wyes Wood, presumably because they overlook the river! At the turn of the seventeenth century, the then Lord of the Manor, Lord Windsor, decided to enclose part of the wood. Local men were employed to dig a large ditch around the site. Understandably, there was much local opposition, and Lord Windsor sought legal help, but to no avail, and the scheme was abandoned. In 1806, parts of the ditch were still in evidence, but now, no trace remains.

Quite a community lived up on this ridge, now only a few cottages are occupied, reached by the forestry roads. The woods are criss-crossed with ancient footpaths edged by stone walls, now thick with moss. There were one or two smallholdings, but most of the residents were woodmen, though the cottages overlooking the Angidy valley were the homes of Wire Workers.

THE TRELLECH ROAD - At the Monmouth end of the village, a road on the left leads to Catbrook and then onto Cleddon and Trellech. On the right, you pass "Orchards", a private house, but once Aubrey Williams' General Stores. Next door is Rose Cottage. Once two cottages, the building has possibly seventeenth century origins. The walls are two feet thick in places, and in the dining room, one of the oak beams has a deeply stopped chamfer, and at one end the beams are supported by stone corbels. There is a spiral stone staircase, which leads to a bedroom with twelve inch wide elm floorboards. The roof timbers are also of elm, with its truss and beams marked with Roman numerals. An old bread oven has been found in the kitchen, and the chimney is big enough for two men to stand in, upright!

Opposite Rose Cottage, just above Rockleigh, there used to be a turners workshop, owned by John Fryer of the Hospice. The power for the machinery was supplied by the Catbrook, which collected in a pond opposite The Woodlands. This pond silted up some seventy years ago. It has been suggested that another, smaller Wire Works existed in the Catbrook Valley, though its possible site has baffled researchers. Maybe there was something on the site of the turnery. Further up the road, there is another pond, at "Steadholm" (the only house in the village to be bombed in the last war), and above that, in the garden of Rockfields, there is a wealth of unexplained stone walls. This cottage, and the neighbouring Forge Cottage, are in an area known as Gurllus Grove, and were originally Foresters Cottages. They, too, are very old and the roof timbers are whole tree trunks, bark, branches and all! Forge Cottage gets its name as being the home of the blacksmith who actually had a Smithy at the Surgery. As horse power was overtaken by the motor car, trade fell, so the Smith built a shed in the garden of his cottage, and established a second Smithy in order to boost his income. Behind these cottages is an area of woodland that stretches down towards the River Wye. Called *Coed Beddick*, which is the Welsh for the wood of Beddick or Buddig. He was father of Docheau (Oudoceus), patron saint of Llandogo. Returning back down the road, towards the village, passing two recently built estates of houses, you will come to the *Pentecostal Church*, built on the site of Fryers' Turnery. When the Ark closed, in the Angidy Valley, in 1922, some members, not wishing to join the Methodist Church, would hold open air services in the grounds of the Abbey, and in bad weather, would meet at the Parva Farmhouse. In time, they heard of a disused corrugated iron building at St Briavels. Jack Jones of the Saw Mill arranged for its collection, and the building was re-erected on this site in the Trellech Road. It was solomonised for marriages in 1929, and the new building that you see today was built in 1969.

ON THE WAY TO MONMOUTH our tour of Tintern now ends, as you rejoin the A466 and head towards Monmouth. Passing the Vineyard, way up on your left, and St Michael's Church on the right, you pass a meadow often flooded at high tide. At the end of this field, near the river, is Tintern Station. Plans for the railway started in 1865, and on the 28 October 1876, a special train left Chepstow to mark the grand opening of The Wye Valley Railway. First stop was Tintern, where the guests lunched, and then on to Monmouth. The return journey was made in the evening, and the valley and Abbey were illuminated with coloured lights. In the 1881 census, no fewer that four of Tinterns' inhabitants were employed at the station. Despite it being a railway passing through some of the most beautiful countryside, the venture was never to be a financial success, even the goods traffic failed to reach expectations, and finally, on the 6 January, 1964, the last train passed through the station. The rails were sold for scrap, and the bridge demolished. Eventually, the site was purchased by the Gwent County Council, and the area was developed to form an Information Centre and Picnic Site, which was opened to the public in September 1975. The project has proved to be very popular, and has given this part of the valley a new lease of life.

Last, but not least, we must mention *The Nurtons*. Once part of the Manor of Tintern Parva, it was sold off as a separate house and grounds in 1889. It was purchased by the Reverend Henry J Williams, Rector of Tintern, who then sold it to Clement Cruttwell, Esq. Once one of the "big houses" in the village, the grounds are now being put to excellent use, growing organic vegetables and herbs.

The road you are on used not to be the way to leave Tintern. The old road, now just a track, passed to the right of the Wye Valley Hotel, up across the fields of Parva Farm, until it dropped down behind the Nurtons, rejoining the river near Brockweir.

TINTERN TODAY

Having talked at length about Tintern's past, it is only right to show that life goes on, and that the village has a present! It is fair to say that the social life is not as rich as it was at the beginning of the century - modern society tends to look towards ready-made entertainment, and the motor car makes it easier to seek pleasure elsewhere.

However, the young are catered for by a Youth Club that meets on a Monday evening, and efforts are being made to start a Christian Youth Group. At the other end of the scale, the older villagers meet on a Tuesday afternoon for talks and outings. The demise of the village school has meant that there are not as many activities for children and their parents as there once was. But the Football Club and Cricket Club still thrive, as they have done for well over a hundred years. Both play in local leagues with some measure of success, and with a great deal of verve! Once, they played at Parva Farm, and at the Reddings, but nowadays, both clubs play on The Leytons, near the Abbey. Hopefully, the Football Club play more "cleanly" than at the match reported in 1889, when, in a match against Brockweir, the game was spoilt by "the rough play and vulgarity" of the opposition, and one of the Tintern players was so badly hurt, he had to be carried home! There is a junior football team, and if the play is as spirited as the noise, they will no doubt be very successful! Nowadays, the wicket leaves a lot to be desired, but once the Tintern Cricket Pitch was graced by none other than the great Welsh player, J. C. Clay.

In the summer, "The Leytons" plays host to the Village Carnival, financed by the Easter Duck Race, and preceded by a procession through the main street. Not so many years ago, "The Leytons" was also the venue for the Tintern Flower Show. This was an important event, equalling the present Chepstow Show. Marquees were erected for the exhibits, races run for the children, and when all was over, a Whist Drive and Dance was held in the evening. Today, the village boasts a Tintern Village Produce Association. This is a society for those interested in gardens and their produce, and came into being just twenty years ago. It is one of fourteen similar groups in Gwent, and is affiliated to Usk College of Agriculture which provides a central venue as well as a fund of expertise. Meetings are held monthly, listening to experts imparting their knowledge during the dark winter evenings, and visiting gardens and garden centres in the summer. Each summer, the Annual Show is held in August.

The Lower Wye Valley is designated an Area of Outstanding Beauty. A group of concerned residents got together in 1968/9, and founded the Lower Wye Valley Preservation Society, with the object of protecting the natural beauty of the Wye Valley between the towns of Chepstow and Monmouth. The Society functions with the help of an elected committee which meets monthly, made up of representatives from the villages of Tutshill, St Arvans, Tintern, Brockweir, St Briavels, Llandogo, Redbrook and Newland. Besides dealing with threats to the enviroment, e.g. from quarry development or wholesale tree-felling, the Committee is consulted by the two District Planning Committees on relevant planning applications. It is also represented on the Joint Advisory Committee, the official body which manages the Area of Outstanding Beauty. The Society acts as a watchdog especially in matters connected with the River Wye, the Woodlands, the roads and inappropriate development, and it attracts the support of all who treasure the rare beauty of the area.

Inevitably, a certain amount of social life is centred around the various Churches, such as the Harvest Supper, Coffee Mornings, Bazaars and Recitals. The other great social venues are the pubs and hotels, of which Tintern has its fair share! The various pubs have Darts Teams which play against each other in Leagues.

So, all in all, this village is still alive and kicking, and glad to share with the visitors all the beauty and history of our community.

BIBLIOGRAPHY

"A History of Monmouthshire - Trellech Hundred", *By Sir Joseph Bradney,* C.B., M.A., F.S.A. *1913*
"Fedw Villages - A Lower Wye Valley History" *By Raymond Howell, Village Publishing 1985*
"An Historical Atlas of Wales from Early to Modern Times"
By William Rees, M.A., D.Sc., F.S.A. Cardiff 1951
"Monmouthshire Medley" Vol 4 *By Reginald Nichols, Village Publishing 1985*
"Tintern Abbey" *By Charles Heath, Monmouth, First Edition 1793 10th Edition 1823.*
"The Monmouthshire Antiquary" *Vol III, Part I, Page 62*
"White Monks in Gwent and the Border" *By David H Williams, Griffin Press 1976*
"Tintern and the Vicinity" *By W H Thomas 1839*
"Ancient Gwent Churches" *By John R Guy, M.A., and Ewart B Smith, M.Sc.*
"Inns and Taverns of Chepstow" *By Ivor Waters, Chepstow Society 1976*
"Leather and Oak Bark at Chepstow" *By Ivor Waters, Chepstow Society, 1970*
"Chepstow Scrapbook" *By Ivor Waters, Moss Rose Press 1986*
"Wye Valley Journal"
"The Scenery of England" *By the Right Hon. Lord Avebury 1906*
"An Anthology of the Wye Valley"
Edited by Stephen Lewis Ingham, The Forest of Dean Newspapers 1972
"The Story of Monmouthshire" Vol I *By Arthur Clarke, M.A., Christopher Davies 1962*
Lines from "Pelleas and Ettarre" *By Alfred, Lord Tennyson*
Lines from "In Memoriam"
"Chepstow - A Poem" *By Edward Davies*
"Collected Poems" *By Masefield*
"Walks in Tintern Woods" *The Forestry Commission*
"Wind and Water Mills", *Journal of the Midland Wind and Water Mill Group, No 9, Page 45*
"A Tide Wheel of Tintern" By Stan Coates
"The Ironworks at Tintern and Sirhowy" *By John Pickin, Gwent Local History, Journal No 52*
"Wood Turning, one of the Vanished Industries of Tintern Forest"
By Mrs Pat Lucas, Presenting Monmouthshire, No 22, Vol II, No 2
"An Industrial History of Tintern" *By Percy G Harris, unpublished, Newport Library*
"The Old Wireworks and Ironworks of Angidy Valley at Tintern"
By H W Paar and D G Tucker, Journal of Historical Metallurgical Society 1975, 9, No 1
"Industry at Tintern" *By D G Tucker*
"The Wireworks Tramway and Bridge at Tintern"
By H W Paar and D G Tucker, Severn And Wye Valley Review, Winter 1973
"Mills, Ponds and other Industrial Sites in the Llandogo and Tintern Parva Area"
By Dr D G Tucker, Severn and Wye Valley Review, Winter 1971
"Our Industrial Past" *By Anthony Burton, National Trust*
"The Old Station Tintern", *Gwent County Council 1989*
"Chepstow Ships" *By Graham Farr. Published jointly by the Chepstow Society and the Newport and Monmouthshire Branch of the Historical Association 1954*
"The Golden Challice" *By L'Estrange Ewen, Newport Library (ref John Callice)*

Sponsors

Grateful thanks to our advertisers, and to our Sponsors listed below, whose generosity has enabled us to reduce printing costs.

Miss L V Mould, Belle Vue House
Mr R A Rastall, Abbey Mill
Mr and Mrs D Phillips
Tintern Carnival Committee
Messrs. A J Karvik and R Chamberlain, Fryer's Row
Mr and Mrs P Howe, Valley House
Mrs E Williams, Laurel Stores

The following recipes came from the book of Thomas Ansley of Redbrook, who became the Quay Master of Brockweir. The first entries date from 1795, and document the many cargoes too and from Brockweir over the following fifty years. Brockweir had close associations with Tintern, (even though it is across the river), particularly as the village had no church of its' own and therefore, the villagers had to travel to Tintern, or other neighbouring parishes, for baptisms, marriages and funerals. It is therefore fairly safe to assume that the recipes were similar to those used in our own village.

Half an ounce of spirits of hartshorn the same quantity of niter. Teaspoonful to be taken at Bedtime. For the Rheumatism.

FOR HOOPING COUGH
2 Scruples Salt of Tarter
2 Scruples Cochineal Powder
To be dissolved in one pint of boiling water.
One tablespoonful to be given when the Cough comes on
(a scruple was an apothecaries' weight of 20 grains)

FOR MAKING BLACKING
½lb of Ivory black
½lb of Treacle
2d worth of sweet oil
1d of oil of Vitorel
1 pint of Vinegar
Mix together